MAXIMIZING, ALLOCATING,
AND PROTECTING
YOUR CAPITAL

BEYOND

the

BA$ICS

SAMMY AZZOUZ

RIVER GROVE
BOOKS

Published by River Grove Books
Austin, TX
www.rivergrovebooks.com

Distributed by River Grove Books

Design and composition by Greenleaf Book Group
Cover design by Greenleaf Book Group
Cover images used under license from
©Shutterstock.com/Kunst Bilder; ©Shutterstock.com/sebos
Figure on page 85 used by permission of RegentAtlantic Capital

Publisher's Cataloging-in-Publication data is available.

Paperback ISBN: 978-1-63299-278-9

Hardcover ISBN: 978-1-63299-280-2

eBook ISBN: 978-1-63299-279-6

First Edition

To Janine,
my best friend and the woman who made it all possible

Contents

Introduction

This is my favorite financial story: In 1952, Walmart founder Sam Walton hired a young man named Willard Walker to run his second store in Fayetteville, Arkansas. It was Walton's first managerial hire, and he enticed Walker with an uninspiring offer: move from Oklahoma and work half days for nothing until the opening while sleeping on a cot in the store.

Walton added one kicker: a share of the store's profits. Walker's then boss scoffed that a share of zero equaled zero and tried to talk him out of it. Walker loved the idea and accepted. Later, when Walton's business became Walmart, Walker again pursued a share of the profits.

He borrowed whatever he could—probably more money than he should've been able to—to buy Walmart stock. Once again, people scoffed. Only this time, that included the Waltons. Sam's brother and business partner, Bud, told Walker that he sure hoped Walker knew what he was doing, because he didn't have as much faith in the stock (and company) as Walker did.

Walker bought more stock than any other Walmart manager. The company experienced tremendous growth. When Walker retired in 1972, his modest lifestyle and stock purchases left him with tens of millions of dollars.

I love this story because it's about becoming wealthy through smart decision-making, the most accessible path to success. You can become rich by founding the next great company (Sam Walton), becoming an investment genius (Warren Buffett), or being a great athlete (Michael Jordan). You could also get hit by lightning three times tomorrow while walking your dog. However, anyone can do it by making better financial decisions, à la Willard Walker.

That's what this book is about: individual capital allocation, using your resources to increase your wealth, and making good decisions with your capital to end up with more. If you already know the financial planning basics, the fundamentals, and the mistakes to avoid but are uncertain of what comes next to increase your wealth, this book is for you.

Most personal finance books fall into one of two categories. Some cover the basics: the smart use of credit cards, debt management, buying a home, how mortgages work, and starting to save early. Some deal with managing your own money by turning you into an investment genius, leaving you under the impression that just by following a few simple formulas or spending a few hours a week, you will beat the pros in an extremely competitive arena. Too few books present what you should pursue beyond the basics to increase your net worth if you are not interested in poring over spreadsheets and reading public company filings.

I wrote this book to help bridge that gap—to provide an individual capital allocation framework for those looking for what to do next to have more money.

WHAT IS CAPITAL ALLOCATION?

Capital allocation is a business concept dealing with a corporation's ability to use its resources (capital) to maximize shareholder wealth. In his fantastic book, *The Outsiders: Eight Unconventional CEOs and Their Radically Rational Blueprint for Success*, William N. Thorndike profiles CEOs who excelled at capital allocation. It's worth reading in full, but one example helps highlight the concept. It's the track record of someone who Warren Buffett himself has said had "the best operating and capital deployment record in American business"—Henry Singleton, CEO of Teledyne.

Google his name and a top result will be a video lecture at the New York Society of Security Analysts by Leon Cooperman, titled "A Case Study in Financial Brilliance: Dr. Henry E. Singleton of Teledyne Inc." Cooperman managed a hedge fund, Omega Advisors, which over a twenty-six-year span outperformed the market by almost 3 percent per year.[1] When brilliant investors call you brilliant, you're damn good.

And Singleton was damn good. Between 1963 and 1990, he delivered a remarkable 20.4 percent compound annual return to his shareholders, compared with 8 percent for the S&P 500.[2]

His company, Teledyne, was one of the 1960s-era conglomerates—companies with many different and unrelated business units. Their stocks were hot back then. They grew by using their own stocks' lofty stock prices to acquire other companies, which drove their stock prices yet higher, enabling them to buy more companies, and so the cycle continued.

---

1   Gara, Antoine. "Know When To Fold 'Em: Billionaire Leon Cooperman To Close Hedge Fund After Big Comeback." Forbes.com. July 23, 2018.

2   William N. Thorndike Jr., *The Outsiders: Eight Unconventional CEOs and Their Radically Rational Blueprint for Success* (Boston: Harvard Business Review Press, 2012), 52.

Singleton made great use of that capital. Instead of buying other expensive publicly traded stocks, he used Teledyne's stock to purchase cheaper, profitable companies. He never overpaid. He focused on generating cash instead of following Wall Street's fascination with quarterly reported earnings, because he believed the best thing for his company's stock was getting more cash for him to allocate effectively. In addition to buying cheap companies, he improved profit margins, reduced capital expenditures, and throughout the 1970s and 1980s, generated a return on assets that Charlie Munger, Warren Buffett's partner and a brilliant investor himself, describes as "miles higher than anybody else . . . utterly ridiculous."[3]

Cash poured into Teledyne's headquarters. Markets are fickle and the love for conglomerates as a category eventually faded. Singleton found himself in a situation where the market price for his company's stock was cheap and other companies were overpriced. Singleton reacted by buying back Teledyne stock. Nowadays, that's not particularly innovative. Indeed, the 2009 through 2019 US stock bull market was partly fed by massive share repurchases. But Singleton was a pioneer who bought back 90 percent of Teledyne's shares.

The repurchases generated a whopping 42 percent compound annualized return, because he was now buying low after selling high. "The average price-to-earnings ratio for Teledyne's stock issuances was over 25; in contrast, the average multiple for his repurchases was under 8."[4]

Singleton's 1980 share buyback was the most impressive. Teledyne's stock was extremely cheap and interest rates in the US had just fallen. He issued bonds to raise capital at a low interest rate

---

3   Thorndike, *The Outsiders*, 45.

4   Thorndike, *The Outsiders*, 47.

and initiated a tender offer to purchase shares. The tender offer was heavily oversubscribed. When interest rates rose and the bonds his company issued to finance the purchase dropped in price, he bought them back and retired the debt at a discount. During this time, he also took advantage of a severe bear market to reinvest the company's insurance portfolio, increasing the total allocation to stocks from 10 percent to 77 percent by 1981.

Why does this matter? Capital allocation concepts like Singleton used can be appropriated by individual investors to help them increase their wealth. A business's main goal is to increase shareholder value. There's a lot of information about the various ways they've attempted it, as well as a quantifiable way to assess those methods. Singleton provides just one example. An individual plugging into this knowledge base and tailoring the most effective corporate capital allocation methods to their own situation can increase their financial success.

That's the good news. The bad news is that it's not easy. You make money by performing your job well, running a good business, and so on. Those endeavors don't necessarily prepare you to allocate the capital you earn well. After all your hard work earning and saving capital, it's worth the effort to learn how to allocate it intelligently. It can ensure that your hard work isn't wasted because you don't know what to do with the fruits of your labor. It will help you achieve important financial goals. It can protect you and your family from financial distress and the impact of tragic events.

Capital allocation provides a framework by which to make all financial decisions. We will appropriate it for individuals through the following tweaks:

TRACKING A DIFFERENT METRIC

Effective corporate capital allocators focus on increasing shareholder value, not growing earnings, hiring more people, building shiny headquarters, or making headlines. We will focus on maximizing your net worth, not how much you make or what you buy.

USING DIFFERENT SOURCES OF CAPITAL

Corporations can use cash produced from their operations, cash raised through debt, or cash raised through stock issuance. Individuals can improve their own cash flow and borrow money.

USING CAPITAL IN DIFFERENT WAYS

CEOs can invest internally in their companies, buy other companies, pay dividends, retire debt, or buy back stock. Individuals can invest in their own education, make investments, pay down their own debt, or consume.

Through all of this, we will not lose sight of the key similarity. It's about optimizing your cash flow and making great decisions with that cash. This book will guide you through that process. It's designed to help someone who has already achieved basic financial success make the correct decisions to increase that success.

Let's begin.

PART 1

Maximizing the Capital Available for Growth

"An investment in knowledge pays the best interest."

—Benjamin Franklin

I remember a conversation with my then wealthiest client over lunch years ago, the patriarch of a $1 billion family. I was thirty, heading in the right direction, but not wealthy by any stretch. The client was talking about selling a plane he had recently purchased and turned to me and said, "Sammy, you have no idea how easy it is to make a million dollars."

I nodded, mumbled something polite, and sat there thinking, "That's easy for a billionaire to say. I have some idea of how hard it is." And then I got it: Making money is easier when you already have money. The client purchased a $30 million plane and sold it for $31 million—a 3 percent gain and an instant $1 million profit.

Anyone can make 3 percent. It's the amount of capital you multiply that gain by that's key.

> To allocate capital, you must have some capital to allocate.

The individual capital allocator's first step toward financial success will be maximizing their own multiplier by learning how to build capital. You can't allocate capital you don't have, and all the brilliant investment strategies in the world won't matter if you're not applying them to enough money.

Building capital typically comes down to three things: maximizing earnings, minimizing spending, and saving on taxes to keep more of what you earn. Each one of those areas will be discussed in its own chapter in this part.

Maximizing earnings will present high-level career advice and review some financial planning basics, so you can continue this journey confident you have them covered.

From there, we will review why it's so important to live below your means as your career success grows. The minimizing spending chapter will review best practices for being cost conscious without sacrificing too much life enjoyment, major spending mistakes to avoid, how to track your spending and why you should, and a case study on why minimizing spending matters so much.

Part 1 will conclude with a look at taxes. All the earning and saving you do won't matter enough if you don't understand how our tax system works and how to minimize taxes and keep more of what you earn. While it's difficult to give specific tax planning advice to a (hopefully) mass audience, I present a tax savings framework we can all use. Its three main components are avoiding things that make your tax situation worse, understanding how taxes work so you're aware of how to minimize your tax bill, and a discussion of some universal tax planning strategies to consider.

CHAPTER 1

Maximizing Your Initial Capital

"Financial literacy is just as important in life as the other basics."
—John W. Rogers Jr.

B efore we can discuss getting beyond the financial planning basics, we should get on the same page regarding those basics. What are the things you should know, the mistakes to avoid, and the smart moves to make before you're ready for the next level? We won't dawdle here, since by purchasing a book with the title *Beyond the Basics*, you're presumably past this stuff. Therefore, we'll keep our list brief and start with an unconventional one you may not have considered.

INVEST IN YOUR CAREER

Your future earnings potential is your most valuable asset. You can earn millions of dollars during your career. Little else will match the financial benefit of maximizing those earnings, so it's worth focusing on your career and skills to take the strongest jump possible into wealth accumulation. Ultimately, the people who best maximize their career opportunities are often the ones most aware of the need to invest in their career.

Arguably the greatest investor of our lifetime, Warren Buffett, says the best investment you can make is in yourself. In a lifetime of making tremendous investments with a track record that would leave other investors salivating, Buffett believes an investment in yourself tops all others.

There are many ways to invest in your career:

- Take a specific class to hone a new skill.

- Pursue a special certification or credential to earn a promotion or enhance your marketability.

- Get that advanced degree to show commitment to your field.

- Volunteer for a different assignment at work to expose yourself to new people and learning opportunities.

- Take a lower-paying job if you will learn a lot from it.

- Find a great mentor and spend time with them.

- Figure out your weaknesses and attack them.

Whatever your path, be cognizant of the need to expend time, money, and effort to develop your long-term skill set. In Buffett's case, an early example is a Dale Carnegie course that he took to fix his crippling fear of public speaking. He credits the class with giving him the confidence to propose to the love of his life a career selling stocks in Omaha. The rest is, as we say, hi

READING

Reading is a career investment. Your career will not be static. You cannot learn everything in school, through a credential, or fast enough at work to accomplish all of your goals. Career development is two-tiered: You master the skills required for your current job while learning new things for the next one. Self-education is key and differentiates those able to get ahead from those who cannot.

Warren Buffett's partner Charlie Munger attributes Buffett's success to—of all things—his reading. "Warren did most of it sitting on his ass and reading. If you want to be an outlier in achievement, just sit on your ass and read most of your life."

Buffett and Munger both view reading as mandatory for financial success. They craved learning and made it a lifelong pursuit since they were never satisfied that they knew enough. From a young age, Buffett "read every business book he could get his hands on."[5] He reads hundreds, if not thousands, of financial statements per year, five newspapers, and numerous magazines and trade journals.

This constant pursuit of knowledge turbocharged his business learning curve. Instead of waiting for school to point out what he should learn, he drove his education and became a successful businessperson while still in high school. And he never stopped reading. The topics changed and the information sources evolved, but

---

5   Roger Lowenstein, *Buffett: The Making of an American Capitalist* (New York: Random House, 2008), 24.

through the decades, he read voraciously to maintain his informational advantage and improve his business acumen.

Of course, he's not the only one. Google "do successful people read" and peruse the articles for yourself. Then again, you're reading this book so your last name is either Azzouz, or I'm preaching to the choir.

For many, reading is a passion they'll pursue in the style they're accustomed. For the rest, I recommend reading more than just technical things related to your job. Balance is essential, and working all day and reading only about work in the evening hinders its achievement. Different subjects will also provide different perspectives that enhance your ability to understand other views, explain concepts better, and learn new things. History, biographies, philosophy, fiction, and science books can all teach important things you can use in your career. Take notes on what you read and apply what you learn as you learn it.

In addition, you should read viewpoints and perspectives you disagree with. You will never learn anything new if you only read what you are predisposed to like. Behavioral economists call it confirmation bias: We search for information validating our viewpoint and ignore anything that doesn't. Think of Fox News and MSNBC. Locking in closes the mind instead of enhancing it.

Don't force yourself to finish something you're not enjoying. There's more out there than there is time to read it, so don't waste time on disappointing material.

NETWORKING

Networking is a career investment. While developing that great career, make sure you're meeting people you can learn from who can help you. It's a hall of fame overused cliché but it's true: It's not what you know; it's who you know. I recommend focusing on both: Invest in a great career by building a strong network and constantly learning.

Developing relationships with people, helping them succeed, and connecting them to others will benefit your career. Some of us are naturals at this. Some of us need direction and help. For that latter group (and really for both since it's a great resource), I would recommend the book *Never Eat Alone: And Other Secrets to Success, One Relationship at a Time* by Keith Ferrazzi. Its core message is that connecting with colleagues and others is a crucial skill set because people do business with people they know and like. It teaches you how to network, provides great examples, and helps you avoid classic networking mistakes.

Don't wait until you need a network to begin thinking about one—start building it now. Set personal networking goals. If you know what you want, you'll have a better sense of who can help you. When I was first starting out as a financial advisor, I worked for a law firm that had a financial advisory practice as a subsidiary. It was a specific job and a specific role; I was a nonpracticing lawyer doing financial planning and business development within a law firm. I feared that if I ever left the firm, there would only be a few other companies interested in my specific background. I made a goal of reaching out to senior people at those companies. Some didn't respond, some I talked to only briefly, some I stayed in touch with, and a couple of years after reaching out, one of them passed my name on to a company looking for someone with my skill set. It proved to be a tremendous opportunity that I would not have been aware of if I didn't set that initial goal.

Stay in touch with your contacts and always follow up any communication. Once you've met them, understand that people need to see you multiple times and hear from you in multiple ways to solidify a relationship. Some people you will contact monthly, some quarterly, and some annually, but create a way for those contacts to happen.

Treat people well. As your network grows, try to think of what you can offer them as well as what you might gain from them. Avoid being known as a schmoozer, a gossip, or a taker. Focus on positive and constructive conversations and relationships. Be known for how nice, smart, and helpful you are, not how juicy you can make a conversation.

Your specific career path will be up to you but focus on traditional education, certification, or credential opportunities; job assignments or mentors that can teach you more; reading to increase your knowledge and perspective; and networking to develop mutually beneficial relationships. Careers need investment and skills need nurturing so that you can consistently grow your income.

GOOD AND BAD DEBT

Good debt is debt that is taken out to buy an important asset, like a home, that should appreciate in value over time and for which the interest rate is reasonable. Right now, the rate on a thirty-year mortgage is about 4 percent; something in that ballpark can safely be called reasonable. Student loans with a reasonable interest rate are good debt, unless the amount that you borrowed will saddle you with hundreds or thousands of dollars of monthly payments for the next twenty to thirty years. The education for your career is a long-term investment and paying off student loans over a decade of earnings is reasonable.

Bad debt is used on things that lose their value over time—pretty much everything you can drive or buy online or that involves a credit card. It's made even worse when the interest rates are really high; credit card debt can have an interest rate as high as 30 percent. Use your credit card for convenience and points, but pay it off every month.

If you're not paying off the balance monthly, you're making a huge mistake. The average credit card interest rate is between 13 percent and 16 percent. Let's split the difference and go with 14.5 percent. Assume you have a minimum payment requirement of 2.5 percent and a $50,000 balance. It would take you 28.4 years to pay off your credit card debt. If you doubled your payment to 4 percent, it would still take more than eight years.

Things that fall in the middle are when you are using debt to buy something like a car and are offered a real low interest rate—say, below that 4 percent mortgage rate. If you would be pulling money out of a portfolio that is earning more than the low interest rate, then you can slide this into the okay debt category and move on.

SAVE FOR THE FUTURE

Once you've patched the holes in your financial ship so you're not leaking capital to high interest rates and bad debt, you can save. Save enough in a short-term bucket to cover any emergencies or planned one-off expenditures. You can then save enough in a mid-term bucket to cover things like a future house down payment, a wedding, and so on—large purchases and life events. Finally, you need to save for the long term: your kids' college education and retirement.

HOW COMPOUND INTEREST WORKS

The final basic for us to get through is compound interest. When an investment generates earnings and those earnings themselves start earning money, that's compounding. A $1,000 investment makes 8 percent in year one (a profit of $80); in year two, your $1,080 dollars also makes 8 percent, but your profit has increased to $86.40. It's a snowball approach to building wealth. It's a basic for many reasons, the biggest of which is that it shows the tremendous value of starting to invest earlier and of packing as much as possible into this snowball to really build mass and momentum.

BEYOND THE BASICS

In the rest of this book, we will move your wealth creation journey beyond the basics, building and customizing the tools of strong corporate capital allocators for individuals. If you understand what we've discussed in this chapter, you're ready for the rest of this book. To summarize:

- Your career earnings can be your largest financial asset. Investing in your career includes education, reading, and networking.
- There is good debt and bad debt, and you need to avoid the worst kind of all: high-interest revolving credit card debt.
- Saving is key, and you need to save for both short- and long-term goals.
- Compound interest is your best long-term friend.

CHAPTER 2

Minimizing Spending

"There is no dignity quite so impressive, and no independence
quite so important, as living within your means."
—Calvin Coolidge

We covered the immense long-term benefit of compounding while discussing the basics, but indulge me one moment longer as I detail a key to this chapter. You invest some money, say $100. It grows by 8 percent in one year to $108. The next year the same 8 percent growth rate earns you $8.64. In year twenty not only has your initial $100 investment more than quadrupled ($431 to be exact), but the dollar profit has basically quadrupled. The 8 percent gain is now paying you $31.98 versus $8.00.

Saving and reinvesting is a great system. Some even think Einstein called it the eighth wonder of the world. But compounding's benefits are limited if you're not saving enough of the financial capital we discussed in the previous chapter. Yes, you understand the basic point that you can't spend more than you earn, but do you realize how aggressive a saver you should be to juice your wealth creation machine? Once you've made money, you need to be vigilant about saving it. Spent capital can't grow. Spend less now so you can have more later. Saving money is a more important skill than making it. Contrary to popular belief, you don't have to make a ton of money to be wealthy. A 2012 survey of millionaires showed that the average millionaire had an income of $89,167, which didn't even put them in the top 20 percent nationally that year, yet their net worth ranked them in the top 4 percent of US households.

Adopt the mindset that a dollar spent today costs significantly more future dollars. It's inverse compounding. Not only have you spent that dollar, but you also lose its future growth. Spending an extra $5,000 per year every year for twenty years doesn't cost $100,000, but another $228,810, assuming that money could have grown by 8 percent annually.

Warren Buffett and Charlie Munger prioritized frugality as a part of building initial capital to grow over time. Buffett looked at every dollar as ten future dollars and hated spending it. If you're working through the math on that, he obviously assumed he could grow his investments at more than 8 percent. That was a safe bet for him.

Munger behaved the same way. He lived below his means to save up enough cash to invest in California real estate, and then to invest alongside Buffett and in his own separate deals. Looking back, he called that initial nest egg accumulation the most difficult part of building his wealth and emphasized that it can only be done one way—by being an aggressive saver.

Let's turn to some ideas on how to do it.

BEING FRUGAL

The independently wealthy got there by saving their money, not by being flashy spenders. Once you understand compounding and the cost of losing capital to its magic effect, you realize it can't happen any other way. Thomas J. Stanley's *The Millionaire Next Door* (co-authored with William D. Danko) and *Stop Acting Rich* provided us with great insight into the spending habits of millionaires. While a bit dated, their statistics pop off the page.

The typical millionaire surveyed by Stanley reported that they never spent more than $399 for a suit and that the owners of $1,000 suits were six times as likely not to be millionaires. Half the millionaires reported that they hadn't spent more than $140 for a pair of shoes or more than $235 for a watch. On average they spent $24,800 for their most recent vehicle and had never spent more than $16 for a haircut (including tip). Only 7.3 percent of them owned a bottle of wine that cost more than $100, and their typical price for dinner out was $20. They sought out value and moderately priced goods.

There are various components to saving money, and for many, it'll always be the most difficult part of the journey, particularly as income grows. Money finds a way to get spent. Wants become needs, which is fine; we only live once and we shouldn't be slaves to the idea of getting wealthier. Just understand it's a trade-off. When you spend, you have less to save. How much you are able to save—and then to invest—will depend on how much you adopt the mindset of making saving money a priority.

CHOOSE YOUR HOME CAREFULLY

A crucial first step in saving more is choosing your home carefully. The best predictor of consumption is your home's value (not income or net worth). A bigger home results in a bigger mortgage, higher property taxes, larger utility and landscaping bills, and more square footage to maintain. The statistics are sobering. For example, nearly three times as many people with investments of more than $1 million live in homes valued at or below $300,000 as are living in homes valued at over $1 million.[6] Consider that for a second. The next time you're driving around the gorgeous suburban development with big houses you can't take your eyes off of, you're three times more likely to find someone with a million-dollar investment portfolio living in a house that costs a fraction of it.

Be thoughtful about where you live. The wrong choice can lead to a lifetime of overspending. Mortgage lenders use a formula to determine loan affordability. The rule of thumb is that your mortgage payment, including real estate taxes and insurance, should not exceed 28 percent of your monthly gross income. For example, if you're making $200,000 per year, 28 percent of your monthly gross income is $4,667. Assuming a 4 percent interest rate, 1.4 percent property tax, and 0.2 percent for insurance, you could afford to buy a $925,000 house and borrow $740,000 after putting down 20 percent. However, the bank isn't saying that's a smart financial planning decision. They're only worried about getting paid back.

Research from *The Millionaire Next Door* provides a better answer: "Never purchase a home that requires a mortgage that is more than twice your household's annual realized income."[7] That

---

6   Thomas J. Stanley and William D. Danko, *The Millionaire Next Door* (New York: RosettaBooks LLC, 2010), Preface.

7   Stanley and Danko, *The Millionaire Next Door*, 67.

would mean a home with a maximum mortgage of $400,000 (twice your $200,000 annual salary). Using the same 20 percent down payment plan means a home worth $500,000 instead of $925,000. Your initial down payment would be $85,000 less. Your monthly payments would be $2,493 instead of $4,612, leading to savings of $25,428 annually. Growing the incremental savings at 5 percent, net of taxes, leads to savings of $1,689,407 for the thirty-year life of the loan. That's a lot of capital that could be allocated to investments. With reasonable returns compounding over time, this decision alone can make the difference of a sizable fortune.

DON'T TRY TO KEEP UP WITH THE JONESES

Much of the benefit of choosing your home carefully results from lower expenses with a cheaper home. However, it also helps protect against a larger potential problem: the tendency to want to keep up with the Joneses. People tend to benchmark themselves against their neighbors and want to own whatever those neighbors do, spending frivolously along with them.

You might trade in your reliable Honda Accord because everyone else is driving big SUVs or luxury cars. When the neighborhood kids get pricier toys, your kids will want their own; your kids will go to more expensive summer camps; they'll play in pricier sports leagues; and you'll hire hitting coaches for baseball. You might send them to private school with their buddies, even though you first moved to this town for its great public schools. You might put in a pool or a nice wine cellar (or both) and join the country club. It happens at every stage of life. Only now, it's happening when you have the money and credit to seriously hinder your future ability to invest.

This is especially true if others perceive you as successful or you're a young professional. Those folks get sucked into the spending game earlier than most. They see bright futures of high incomes ahead of them, move into those nicer neighborhoods at a younger age, and spend to keep up with everyone else.

This is aspirational wealth, and it impedes your ability to create real wealth. In order to build capital to later allocate to investment, you have to avoid burning through it now. It doesn't matter what your neighbors have; what matters is what you are able to grow from what you have.

TRACK YOUR SPENDING

How do you know how much you're spending and saving unless you keep track of it? How can you improve without a starting point? What spending categories contribute the most to your overall costs? You also need an accurate spending number to build a financial plan.

Track your expenses, at least temporarily, to know where your money is going. Defense against spending wins championships, so do it long enough to get solid information about your spending habits in order to make improvements. And if you don't continue tracking every week, month, or year, revisit it often enough to keep your numbers accurate.

My wife and I track our expenses through Mint.com. It's a straightforward interface that links your bank accounts, credit cards, investment accounts, retirement accounts, mortgages, real estate, and so on through its secure site. Once you're set up, it updates your information whenever you log in. You'll see what you're spending and learn that there are only a few categories of spending that really matter—probably mortgage, vacation, groceries, and eating out. Most of your work creating savings should focus on the bigger categories, but be cognizant of everything.

Tracking allows you to find any smaller things worth attacking like recurring monthly expenses for items you don't use or need. It can also reassure you about the small indulgences you take that don't add up to much. The first time I did this, I expected to find that I spent way too much money at Dunkin' (I am from Boston after all). Good news: I didn't. But the process did reveal some larger items I was able to work on.

SPENDING: A CASE STUDY

Let's compare two saving and spending plans by similarly situated families. Joe's and Jim's lives are identical on paper (earnings, portfolio returns, ages, income and property tax rates, and savings opportunities), except for their personal consumption.

Joe and Jim were both born in 1977, began working in 2000, and share the following earnings graph.

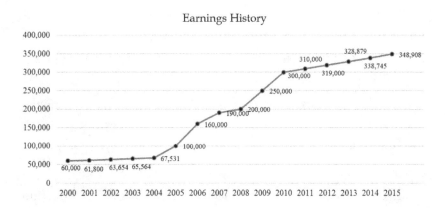

Earnings History

Joe and Jim each spent $44,000 per year (increased annually by 3 percent inflation) from their salaries between 2000 and 2004. They both rented their homes and made annual retirement contributions of 8 percent to a 401(k) and $2,000 to a Roth IRA. Things changed in 2005, when their pay jumped to $100,000.

Joe bought a nice house in a solid middle-class neighborhood for $250,000, with 20 percent down and a 6 percent mortgage. He started spending $7,500 more because he could afford it. Joe's total 2005 spending related to his home and lifestyle increased to $66,000. He also increased his Roth IRA contributions to $3,000.

Jim started spending more in 2005 as well. He didn't think Joe's neighborhood was nice enough and found a new development. He paid for crown molding even though he didn't know what it was, bought Viking appliances even though his wife hated cooking, and convinced himself he needed a bigger house than Joe's even though their families are the same size. Jim's house cost $400,000; his mortgage was $320,000; and his property taxes, maintenance, and expenses were higher than Joe's. Almost immediately, Jim started to keep up with the Joneses and added $15,000 to his annual budget to buy Ethan Allen furniture, a whole-house entertainment system, a wine fridge, a bigger grill, and so on.

In 2006, Joe was tired of driving his ten-year-old Nissan Sentra with a broken tape deck, so he bought a fully loaded Toyota Camry for $28,000. He also increased his Roth IRA contributions to $4,000.

Jim also went car shopping in 2006 but couldn't fathom the idea of a Camry. He ended up with a BMW 3 Series instead, which cost $45,000. Jim didn't contribute to his Roth that year, or any other year.

In 2007, Joe's family took a nice vacation, costing $10,000, and

Joe again contributed $4,000 to his Roth IRA. Jim put a wine cellar in his basement, at a cost of $15,000. His family vacation that year also cost $15,000.

In 2008, the purse strings loosened up again, and both Joe and Jim increased their spending by $10,000. That year, Jim joined the country club. His total extra spending was $15,000. And in 2009, Jim became the fourth person in his neighborhood to install a pool, for $40,000.

After 2009, both families' expenses increased by 3 percent per year. Anything not spent in a given year was saved in a portfolio invested in global stocks.

I'm sure you've figured out that, by the end of 2015, Joe had saved more money than Jim, but how big do you think the difference was? Jot it down in percentage or dollar terms, and see if you're right.

Jim had $1,209,000. Joe had $2,120,000. Simply by avoiding overspending, Joe saved an additional $911,000—that's 75 percent.

MULTIPLE FUTURE DOLLARS

Whenever I meet families interested in working with me, I ask them how they've achieved their financial success. Typically, the answer is some variation of controlling spending and living below their means. One couple answered that they cut each other's hair. This was a figurative mindset, not their literal approach. No one has ever said, "By spending whatever I want as my pay increased."

Once you understand compounding and the idea that a dollar spent today costs multiple future dollars, you're already adopting the mindset needed to retain capital for future growth. From there, be wary of temptations. Purchase the home you need, not the one you can afford. Spend to meet your family's needs, not because others are doing it. And track your expenses at least occasionally to give yourself the information necessary to improve.

CHAPTER 3

Minimizing Taxes

"The hardest thing in the world to understand is the income tax."
—Albert Einstein

Minimizing taxes is crucial; it allows you to keep more of what you earn and save. It doesn't do your capital compounding machine much good to earn a bunch of income, be disciplined enough to save it, and then watch it leak away to bad tax planning. This process won't be easy, but we should focus on it for a few reasons.

First, here's how our tax system works: You earn income through the year but don't prepare your taxes until the year is over. By then, the tax consequences of your actions are mostly locked in (except for some types of retirement contributions you are allowed to make after the year is over), and you've lost the opportunity to lower your tax bill through planning. Understanding how taxes work is important so you don't unnecessarily increase your tax bill and so you know when to reach out for help during the year.

Second, most people don't receive enough tax planning advice. Tax planning advice is different from tax preparation. Tax prep can cost a few hundred to a thousand dollars, a fee that covers complying with the tax code by filing your returns. The preparers are under a massive time crunch, since they don't get all the information they need to file the returns early enough and have to prepare many returns in a short time. They're charging a fair fee for the amount of time and expertise it takes to prepare your returns. You won't receive much else, since most haven't built into that prep fee the cost to review and explain your return, discuss missed planning opportunities, and set you up for a better year. They're not building into their fee an annual check-in meeting or a year-end meeting to discuss opportunities. The tax planners who do this charge more. People are often reluctant to pay for that extra advice. It's a big missed opportunity to improve your financial situation, and I would recommend finding someone who will do planning and prep. Until then, hopefully this chapter will help.

Hiring the right tax advisor connects to the third reason. Even if you are working with someone who does both, more tax awareness on your end will ensure you reach out to your tax advisor at the right times. People often blame their CPA or tax preparer for tax surprises or missed opportunities that they learn about after the fact. However, if your CPA or preparer doesn't know what's going on during the year, they can't provide proactive advice. Greater understanding on your end of what they need to know will help them deliver better outcomes.

THE FRAMEWORK FOR SUCCESSFUL TAX PLANNING

My goal in this chapter is to provide a general tax savings framework to start you on the path to keeping more of what you earn. The framework has three parts. First is learning to avoid things that needlessly lead to higher tax bills, which we'll call doing no harm. You'll then learn how the tax rules work, so you're in a better position to reduce your tax bite as you allocate capital and make money. We will wrap up with a review of specific tax planning opportunities you should be aware of.

FIRST, DO NO HARM

Doing no harm means not making your tax bill higher by unnecessarily realizing income. You'll owe taxes on the income you generate. Let's just not make it worse.

At the risk of oversimplifying, we are taxed on realized income and not net worth increases. That may be a confusing distinction, so let's clarify with some examples.

When you earn money, you are taxed. Let's say you sold a product or provided a service. If you earned $15, you're taxed on that income. You'll lose some percentage of that income, so your net worth increases not by $15 but by $15 minus the taxes. If your income tax rate is 30 percent, then your net worth has increased by $10.50.

However, if a stock you own increases in price from $10 to $15, you have a $5 profit, but that profit isn't taxed until you sell the stock. Your net worth increased by $5, but since you didn't realize the income by selling the stock, there's no tax due. If you sell the stock, just like earned income, you get taxed: The $15 becomes $14 (or a bit less), assuming prevailing capital gains rates. Your net worth increased, but you lost 20 percent (or more) of that increase to taxes. It's the same math with a stock that paid a dividend of $5 instead of appreciating by $5. The dividend is taxable because you received it, leaving you with, again, $14 instead of $15. Which situation would you rather be in if you're trying to minimize taxes and increase net worth?

Do no harm means maximizing your unrealized income and minimizing realized income as your net worth grows. We're talking about maintaining an uninterrupted compounding machine. Minimizing realized income keeps more of your capital working, since it will not face immediate taxation. Financially successful people do this well. The typical millionaire next door has less than 7 percent of their wealth taxed every year, while the average American household pays 11.6 percent of their net worth annually in income tax (typically their largest expense).[8] It's a stunning difference that I want you to be on the right side of, particularly since it's so easy to do. We're not talking about smoke-filled rooms, offshore accounts, tax shelters, Swiss bankers, or fancy loopholes and nonsense. Instead, you're going to realize less income by spending less and being a long-term investor.

MINIMIZE REALIZED INCOME

You cannot minimize realized income if you constantly need money to fund your spending needs. To spend a lot, you must do one of two things that will hurt. Either you're going to consistently realize income (e.g., dividend-paying stocks, bonds that pay interest, and rental properties), or you'll constantly be selling investments and realizing gains to fund your lifestyle. Either way, you will not be

---

8   Thomas J. Stanley and William D. Danko, *The Millionaire Next Door* (New York: RosettaBooks LLC, 2010), 54.

setting up a structure to allow net worth increases to remain unrealized and untaxed. You won't be letting enough capital marinate in your long-term compounding machine.

MAXIMIZE UNREALIZED INCOME

Long-term capital gains are taxed at either 15 percent or 20 percent federally (depending on which tax bracket you are in). Short-term capital gains are taxed at your marginal ordinary income tax rate, which can be as high as 37 percent. Your state may also have a higher capital gains tax for your short-term gains, as mine does. The least tax-efficient thing you can do is to sell appreciated stocks within a year of purchase because then they're taxed as ordinary income instead of as capital gains. Holding on to the investment for at least a year can reduce your tax bill by half.

Now, this is where you might shake your head and scold me for letting the tax tail wag the dog. Perhaps you have some other investment clichés to trot out like telling me not to catch a falling knife or to buy low and sell high. Of course, I don't want you holding on to bad investments for tax reasons. However, a holding period of at least a year should be your goal.

Beyond that initial goal of at least a one-year holding period to qualify for the long-term capital gains rate on your gains, you can avoid further tax harm by having longer holding periods. When we reach the section on allocating capital, one option will be a traditional stock and bond portfolio. Frequent trading in your portfolio pleases the IRS, because you realize gains and pay taxes on them. Long-term investors make fewer trades, keep their gains unrealized, and pay less in taxes. That leads to more capital being compounded, since these investors are not losing a piece of the iceberg every year to taxes.

Higher turnover leads to less long-term capital, since turnover generates taxable income. Therefore, lower turnover is preferable. One investment legend goes so far as to claim it can add up to 3 percent per year to your returns. Charlie Munger explained that when you buy and hold a stock, "if it works, the governmental tax system gives you an extra one, two, or three percentage points per annum with compound effects."[9]

Let's review the math and see. We'll begin by examining the effects of different turnover rates on a hypothetical portfolio, then turn to real examples using mutual funds and show you how to research the tax efficiency of different investments yourself before buying.

Our hypothetical portfolio will be $100,000, will have an annual 9 percent return based on price appreciation (no dividends), and will face a long-term capital gains tax rate of 20 percent. Our holding period is twenty years.

Turnover rate	Final portfolio value
0%	$560,441
25%	$520,711
50%	$474,803
75%	$440,874
100%	$401,694

9   Janet Lowe, *Damn Right! Behind the Scenes with Berkshire Hathaway Billionaire Charlie Munger* (New York: John Wiley & Sons).

As you can see, deferring your capital gains taxes through lower turnover provides tremendous value. Any increase in turnover leads to less wealth. While we don't quite reach Munger's 3 percent, the difference in net return between the 0 percent turnover portfolio and the 100 percent turnover portfolio is 1.8 percent. Over twenty years, that equates to the 0 percent turnover portfolio being 39.5 percent larger than the 100 percent one.

It's true that the 0 percent turnover portfolio has a significant amount of embedded gains that it'll still have to pay taxes on—$460,441, to be exact—and the 100 percent turnover portfolio does not, since all taxes were paid annually. However, even after paying those taxes, the 0 percent turnover portfolio will have $468,353 versus the $401,694 in the 100 percent turnover portfolio. It pays to be a patient investor in more ways than one.

That's the concept. Now, let's turn to implementation. You can access a stock portfolio in two primary ways. The first is directly through individual stocks. The second is indirectly, through hiring someone to manage your money. The second avenue can be further split into a manager who will buy and sell individual stocks for you or for a pooled vehicle like a mutual fund, where you will only see the number of shares you own in that pooled vehicle. Both ways allow you to focus on low turnover strategies, albeit via different routes.

The first is the easiest. If you're investing directly and on your own in individual stocks or exchange-traded funds (ETFs, pooled vehicles that invest in individual securities, like stocks and bonds, and trade like stocks, meaning they can be bought and sold on stock exchanges) and want to maintain a low turnover strategy, your complete control of the portfolio allows for it. Bear in mind that I'm not recommending that you manage your own portfolio (or the opposite, that you don't)—but we'll discuss that further in part 2. Right now, I'm just discussing how to implement a low turnover trading strategy.

The second method gets a bit more involved and, as I mentioned, splits into two avenues. You can hire a money manager. If they have the authority to make investment decisions in your account without consulting you first (a discretionary money manager), you will need to know their portfolio turnover rates before hiring them to make sure they fit your criteria. You can't expect them to be at or near 0 percent turnover; however, it is reasonable to expect them to have a turnover rate below 50 percent, and even closer to 15 percent to 25 percent. Remember, a 50 percent turnover means their average holding period for a stock is two years. That's not long-term investing; 25 percent is four years, which is more like it.

If you don't hire a money manager, you can still get someone to manage your portfolio through purchasing an investment vehicle like a mutual fund, which pools people's money together and has a manager or management team invest the money for shareholders.

Similar to working with a money manager, you implement a low turnover strategy with a mutual fund by researching the turnover before purchasing. That information is easy to find online.

The investment research website Morningstar takes this tax analysis one step further by providing what they call a *tax cost ratio* (how much of the fund's return was lost annually to taxes) for mutual funds. They have information for each fund that shows the fund's pretax return, posttax return, and tax cost ratio. You can compare the numbers of the fund you're considering to any other mutual fund. You can also compare the fund to its own category to know if it is above or below average in tax efficiency. The information and tools are available to access a low turnover portfolio no matter your investment path. Use them. This is not only good tax planning advice; it's good investment advice.

Invest; don't trade. It's important to understand the difference. When you buy a stock (or a basket of stocks), you should do so because you believe in the long-term business prospects of that company (or companies). That's investing. Don't buy a stock because you think you can predict a price increase. That's trading. It's speculative, impossible to do consistently, and tax inefficient. Patience is a crucial investment virtue.

Ben Graham, Warren Buffett's mentor and the godfather of security analysis, said that "any contemplated holding period shorter than a normal business cycle (typically three to five years) is speculation."[10] Buying a stock is buying a piece of a business. The economic rewards from that business will take time to realize, and a proper evaluation of that business requires seeing it perform through different phases of the business cycle: good times, bad times, and everything in between.

Research from *The Millionaire Next Door* supports this. Only about 9 percent of the millionaires Stanley and Danko interviewed failed to retain their investments for that one-year period; 42 percent had made no trades at all in the year prior to the interview.[11]

Putting this all together will help you keep more of what you earn by focusing on what you can control. Focus on increasing your net worth without realizing income. You are not taxed on a net worth increase unless that increase is triggered by realizing taxable income. Spend less, so you won't need income-generating investments or to sell investments at a gain to fund your lifestyle. Invest for the long term. Don't sell appreciated investments within a year of purchase,

10 Joe Carlen, *The Einstein off Money: The Life and Timeless Financial Wisdom of Benjamin Graham* (New York: Prometheus Books, 2012), 127.

11 Stanley and Danko, *The Millionaire Next Door*, 67.

because you'll face a higher tax bill. Hopefully, you can take it well beyond that and structure a low turnover portfolio to keep more of your capital exposed to long-term returns.

UNDERSTAND THE TAX RULES

Step two in our tax planning framework is understanding how income tax works—at a high level since I have no interest in putting you in a coma. A great way to understand tax rules is walking through Form 1040, the federal form individuals use to file their returns. It's not easy. The instructions alone are 114 pages. We'll go slow and skip a lot.

You start by reporting income, which is easy enough to understand. A couple of surprises or noteworthy reminders are below. Remember that income is a catchall category. The IRS wants to know all that you made. That includes foreign income; tips; disability insurance payments from policies you didn't pay for; interest, dividends, and capital gains; individual retirement account (IRA), pension, and annuity distributions; and unemployment compensation and Social Security benefits. Then there's the catchall category, which includes prizes and awards, jury duty pay, reimbursements for deductions you took in other years, gambling winnings, lottery payouts, and canceled debts. Note that if you made nondeductible IRA contributions—you contributed to the IRA, didn't get the tax deduction, but the proceeds grew tax deferred, and now you are taking withdrawals—the contributions aren't taxed again. Dollars contributed to a retirement plan through salary deferrals, such as a 401(k) plan, are not reported as W-2 income.

Items that reduce your income to your adjusted gross income

(AGI) come next. The more common adjustments are health savings account deductions and other deductions relating to self-employment, alimony paid, and deductible IRA contributions.

From there, you get to take deductions from your income. You have the choice of taking the standard deduction or your itemized deductions. If you itemize your deductions and the total comes to more than the IRS gives you for a standard deduction amount, you use that higher amount.

It's a convoluted list, but here are the biggies:

- Retirement plan contributions if you are self-employed
- Medical and dental expenses, but only if they're greater than 7.5 percent of your adjusted gross income
- State and local taxes you paid like income or general sales tax, real estate tax, and personal property tax, subject to a cap of $10,000
- Home mortgage interest—any loan secured by your first or second home, including your first and second mortgages and home equity loans, subject to certain caps
- Charitable gifts

Congratulations, you have your taxable income and are one step removed from figuring out how much tax you owe. Except it's one huge step with a bunch of twists and turns. Let's cut to the chase as much as possible.

So far, we've treated all of your income equally. The IRS needs to know your total income for a variety of reasons. However, calculating the total tax you owe requires considering the different sources of income.

SCHEDULE D

Use Schedule D to calculate the capital gains tax. A capital gain or loss is generated when you buy and sell a capital asset. Common capital assets are stocks, bonds, mutual funds, real estate, business property, and other financial instruments (such as options and commodity derivatives). Schedule D will also have you punch in gains or losses from partnerships, S corporations, and estates and trusts.

Schedule D distinguishes between short-term gains and losses and long-term ones (investments held for more than a year). You first net your short-term transactions against each other, then your long-term ones, and then you net them against each other. A net short-term gain will be taxed at your ordinary income tax rate. A net long-term capital gain will be taxed at 15 percent or 20 percent. Either kind of loss up to $3,000 can be used to reduce your income that year. Anything in excess of $3,000 is carried over to future years. Gains on collectibles are taxed at 28 percent.

After figuring out the Schedule D tax, you figure out the tax on your regular income. We're two steps away, but the next one is annoying.

ALTERNATIVE MINIMUM TAX

Perhaps you've heard of the alternative minimum tax (AMT)? It used to be a much bigger deal than it is now. Google it and you'll get plenty of sob stories saying it was created ages ago to make sure rich people couldn't avoid income tax. But when it was created, an inflation adjustment didn't get added, so more people were captured by it. The most recent income tax bill addressed this, so we are seeing fewer people caught by it. For now, let's just say that you calculate what you owe under the regular system and then calculate your AMT, and if the AMT system is higher, you pay more.

CREDITS

With AMT out of the way, you next take any tax credits you're allowed. Then you add in other taxes you must pay, like self-employment tax (if applicable), and calculate what you've already paid in taxes during the year. You'll either owe more or get a refund.

That's a general federal income tax overview. Now we can transition to step three of our framework—specific tax planning advice.

TAKE ADVANTAGE OF SPECIFIC PLANNING OPPORTUNITIES

Now that you've mastered doing no harm and understand how the tax rules work, let's turn to the final piece of our tax planning framework: highlighting specific planning opportunities available to you as an individual. Some of these are reiterations of things mentioned earlier: You should avoid short-term capital gains and reduce portfolio turnover. Beyond those simple strategies, you can take advantage of tax-sheltered retirement plans.

The retirement plan rules in our country are unnecessarily complex. There are different kinds of plans, all with their own names, which work in different ways, with different contribution limits. As an employee, it's a bit easier to navigate this maze, since all you need to do is make sure that you're contributing the maximum you're allowed to the retirement plan your employer provides. Every dollar you contribute reduces your taxable income by that amount. If your taxable income is reduced by a dollar and the rate at which you are effectively taxed is 30 percent, you have saved $0.30 by contributing that dollar to the retirement account.

Things get more complicated when you're the employer responsible for figuring out which retirement plan and design to choose for your company's needs. You need to understand (or work with someone who does) the different plans, design options, and how they work. Different plan types come with different contribution limits, different funding requirements for your employees, different costs—basically, different everything that matters. You'd think our retirement plan system would be easy, in that there would be one set amount everyone is allowed to contribute into one type of plan. It isn't, but we can figure it out.

DEFINED CONTRIBUTION PLANS

There are three main defined contribution (DC) plans to consider as a business owner:

- Simplified employee pension plan (SEP IRA)
- Savings incentive match plan for employees (SIMPLE IRA)
- 401(k) plan

The following table highlights the differences between the plans through the lens of the business owner looking to save on taxes.

Plan Type	Contribution Limit	Catch-up over-50 Contribution
SEP IRA	$57,000	$0
SIMPLE IRA	$13,500	$3,000
401(k) employee deferral	$19,500	$6,500
Maximum 401(k) contribution, including employer contribution	$57,000	$63,000

The SEP IRA is the easiest to set up and allows for a maximum contribution of $57,000. However, an employer has to contribute the same percentage of income they used for their own contribution for all employees. This makes it more costly to run if you have employees. In addition, you have to make a certain amount to get that maximum contribution per the SEP IRA funding rules.

The SIMPLE IRA allows a maximum contribution of $13,500 plus a 3 percent match, which is much lower than the SEP IRA. The SIMPLE IRA allows catch-up contributions, where people over fifty are allowed to make larger contributions ($3,000).

A 401(k) is more costly to set up and administer, but it allows a maximum salary deferral of $19,500. This type of plan also allows catch-up contributions (up to $6,500 per year). In addition, employers can provide matching contributions and pair the 401(k) with a profit-sharing plan. The maximum you can contribute into your combined 401(k) and profit-sharing plan is $57,000 (or $63,000 if you're over fifty). If you're looking to maximize contributions and get flexible plan design, the 401(k) is unbeatable, because of the creative ways you can structure your profit-sharing plan.

Profit-sharing plans allow employers to make discretionary contributions annually to employee retirement accounts (including owner-employees). There is no required contribution amount, and it doesn't have to be done annually. Contributions are made under a set formula, which can be created to benefit the company owners by distributing a larger percentage of the profit-sharing contributions to them. This makes it cheaper than a SEP IRA to get contributions to the $57,000 maximum if you have employees.

Profit-sharing plans do not always require the same percentage contribution for all employees. If, as the employer, you want to contribute enough to hit the maximum limit of $57,000 or $63,000, but you do not want to make that contribution for everyone else, it's allowed. The rules allow you to set up groups of employees within the company and contribute different percentages to the groups;

this is called cross-testing. The profit-sharing benefits can be skewed to a certain group that includes you, allowing you to make larger personal contributions a lot more cheaply than you would think.

Different plans are available to shelter income for business owners. You should shelter as much as you can afford in order to save on taxes and diversify your wealth. Picking the right plan and plan design is essential, as is picking the right plan provider. Most of the cheap 401(k) options available to you don't have the plan design expertise needed to set up an advanced profit-sharing plan. Even those plans provided by the biggest names out there may not be capable of creating a cross-tested profit-sharing plan. Find one who is.

DEFINED BENEFIT PLANS

If your business is thriving and you do not want to be bound by the plan limits mentioned above, you can go well beyond them by setting up a defined benefits (DB), or pension, plan. DC plans target a defined contribution to a retirement account and whatever those contributions grow to in the future is what your retirement account will be. DB plans target a defined future benefit and use actuarial assumptions to figure out what contributions are needed each year to reach that future benefit. It's a complicated analysis, which is one reason why DB plans are more costly to set up and administer than DC plans. The other reason is that the contributions are employer paid. However, they can more than make up for that increased cost by facilitating large tax-deductible retirement contributions, which can be well in excess of DC plan limits and can reach hundreds of thousands of dollars. A DB plan can also be paired with a DC plan so you can benefit from both approaches and tax breaks.

Since DB plans target a defined future benefit and not a defined contribution, the maximum that you can contribute is expressed in terms of a maximum annual benefit during retirement. That benefit can't exceed the lesser of 100 percent of your average compensation for your three highest-paid years or $230,000.

One type of DB plan, called a cash balance plan, is a bit of a hybrid, since the benefit is expressed more like a DC plan in that the target benefit is a stated future account balance.

INDIVIDUAL RETIREMENT ACCOUNTS

An individual retirement account or IRA is a type of account that provides tax benefits for retirement savers. Everyone with earned income, or whose spouse has earned income, is eligible to contribute to one. The annual contribution limits are currently $6,000 ($7,000 if you are fifty or over). These limits are inflation adjusted.

There are two types of IRAs—traditional and Roth. It's important to first understand how they work and differ from each other before turning to a discussion of how you should be using them in your wealth management plan.

Traditional IRA

Contributions to a traditional IRA are fully tax deductible if you and your spouse are not covered by a retirement plan at work or if you are covered at work but come under certain income thresholds. These are based on modified adjusted gross income, which is basically your AGI with certain rarely used deductions added back. For single tax filers, that threshold is $65,000 for a full deduction, although if you make between $65,000 and $75,000, you can receive a partial deduction. For married filers, those numbers are $104,000 for full deductibility and partial deductibility between $104,000 and $124,000. You can still make a contribution if you're eligible but earn more than these income thresholds applicable to your situation. It just won't be fully tax deductible.

The investments within an IRA grow tax deferred, meaning you do not pay tax on the account's annual earnings. However, when you withdraw from the IRA, your deductible contributions and earnings are taxed as regular income. Nondeductible contributions are not taxed when they are withdrawn, so long as you keep track of them through Form 8606 on your tax return.

Required minimum distributions must begin when you turn 72 and can start penalty free after 59½ (or earlier under certain exceptions).

Roth IRA

Contributions to a Roth IRA are not tax deductible. You can contribute to one if you have earned income or if your spouse does, but eligibility is subject to strict income limits. Single tax filers need to earn less than $124,000 and are partially eligible if their income is between $124,000 and $139,000. Married filers need to earn less than $196,000 and are partially eligible if their income is between $196,000 and $206,000.

Investments in a Roth IRA grow tax-free, which is a key differentiator from the traditional IRA's tax-deferred growth. Roth IRA distributions are completely tax-free. You never pay tax on the earnings. The original owner of the Roth IRA is also not required to take required minimum distributions like they are with the traditional IRA.

How to use IRAs

The standard advice is that, if you're eligible for both IRA types, you should contribute to a traditional IRA if you think your future tax rate will be lower or the same as it is now and to a Roth IRA if you expect your rate to be higher. To maximize your wealth, it's best to pay taxes at the lowest possible rates; if your future tax rate will be higher, you will want a tax break then as opposed to now, at the lower rate.

Those just starting their careers, who don't make a lot of money, or who are at their peak earnings in a well-paid profession can have a strong sense of their future tax rate relative to their current rate. For the rest of us, it's tough to predict multiple decades into the future. So let's simplify.

If you're eligible to contribute to a deductible traditional IRA or to a Roth IRA, and if your income falls in the top three tax brackets (37 percent, 35 percent, and 32 percent), you should take your tax break now; that is, you should get your tax-deductible contribution now. If your income falls below these brackets, you should forgo the tax deduction for future tax-free Roth distributions.

If you're not eligible to make a tax-deductible contribution to a traditional IRA but can contribute to a Roth IRA, do the Roth.

If you aren't eligible to contribute to a deductible traditional IRA or to a Roth IRA, what you do depends on a few things. If you do not already have any IRA assets, you can make what is known as a backdoor Roth IRA contribution. You make a nondeductible traditional IRA contribution, then convert the traditional IRA to a Roth IRA. This possibility was set up because people typically had deductible contributions or deferred earnings in traditional IRAs and the conversion to a tax-free Roth would require the deductible contributions and deferred earnings to be realized as income and, therefore, taxed. The IRS gets revenue now instead of perhaps decades in the future.

Please note that this only works if you don't have money in an IRA already. That includes traditional IRAs, rollover IRAs, and SEP IRAs. Account types you do not have to worry about are employer-sponsored retirement plans like 401(k)s, 403(b)s, and profit-sharing plans. Inherited IRAs also do not count.

What happens if you ignore the rules on existing IRA assets and try to convert only a new cash nondeductible IRA contribution to a Roth IRA? The pro-rata rule applies. It works by combining all of your IRA balances and taxing you on the pro-rata percentage of your IRA balances, essentially forcing the taxation of a portion of your IRA accounts that you were not trying to convert.

If you do have IRA assets you don't want to convert, you could consider a nondeductible IRA contribution. Yes, there's no tax deduction, but the earnings grow tax-deferred, and if you properly keep track of the nondeductible contributions on Form 8606 of your federal tax return, you will not owe tax on the aggregate nondeductible contributions when your funds are withdrawn. It's not easy to say whether you should do this or not. On the plus side, you get more money growing tax-deferred, which provides a long-term benefit. However, in the future, those earnings will be taxed as ordinary income. If you forgo the nondeductible IRA contributions and add that money to your brokerage account, the earnings will be taxed every year, but they will be taxed at lower tax rates (remember our capital gains and dividends discussion). I have also seen many people lose track of the nondeductible contributions they have made. At the end, I don't have a firm recommendation without knowing your particular situation, but it's an option you should be aware of.

HEALTH SAVINGS ACCOUNT

Enroll in a high-deductible health plan and contribute the maximum allowed to a health savings account. There's currently a trend toward consumerism to address the rising costs of health care. The idea is that if more people are incentivized to be smart health-care consumers, health-care costs will somehow become cheaper. This trend, while putting more responsibility on individuals, provides those individuals with a tax planning opportunity if they participate in a certain type of health plan with lower premiums and higher deductibles, although the participants face larger potential out-of-pocket health-care costs. To offset this detriment, the high-deductible plans can be paired with a health savings account (HSA) that employers and employees can contribute to. The maximum contribution limits are $7,100 for a family and $3,550 for an individual.

HSA contributions are considered "triple tax-free," meaning the contributions are made with pretax dollars, the account earnings grow tax-free, and withdrawals for qualified medical expenses are tax-free. Additionally, after the age of sixty-five, you can withdraw from an HSA for any reason but only pay tax on the gains if the withdrawals are not for qualified medical expenses. Think of it as an additional retirement plan contribution. It's like a Roth IRA for health care, except you get a tax deduction on the way in. Even if you decide to spend money out of it every year as you work toward your deductible limit, you are still better off making the contribution because of the tax deduction.

If you can enroll in a high-deductible plan with an HSA, you should. If that is the only option you have, maximize your contributions to the HSA. Consider letting the money in the HSA grow and paying health-care expenses in your younger working years out of pocket.

CHARITABLE CONTRIBUTIONS

Charitable gifts are tax-deductible, and you can make smarter charitable contributions by donating appreciated stock directly to charities or to a donor-advised fund. You could give $1,000 to the local Boys & Girls Club; deduct $1,000 from your income; and if you are in the 38.8 percent combined marginal tax bracket, save nearly $400 in taxes. If instead of donating cash, you donated shares of XYZ Corp that you had initially purchased for $500 over a year ago that are now worth $1,000, your total tax benefit would be higher. You would still get a deduction of $1,000 and realize nearly $400 in tax savings. In addition, you wouldn't be on the hook for the capital gains tax, since the charity sells the stock. In this example, the gain is $500. Let's say your capital gains tax rate is 23.8 percent. The tax on a $500 gain is $118. Add that to $400, and you get a tax savings of more than half of your contribution, significantly better than donating cash.

PAY FOR ADVICE

A good tax advisor will help you navigate this tax planning framework, partner with you on executing proper tax reducing strategies, save you the time and hassle of figuring this out on your own, and prevent expensive mistakes. Find someone who works with people like you (e.g., corporate executive, physician, small business owner, etc.), does not simply prepare taxes but discusses planning strategies as well, and comes with a recommendation from someone you know and trust. The tax code is too complex to go it alone.

Now that you've learned the framework for successful tax planning—doing no harm, understanding the tax rules, and taking advantage of specific planning opportunities—you will be better positioned for minimizing taxes and keeping more of what you earn. This will be accomplished through a combination of structuring investments correctly to increase your net worth without unnecessarily realizing income, avoiding mistakes that can make your tax bill worse, and taking advantage of all the tax-deferred and tax-free vehicles available to you. It'll also make you a better consumer of tax planning advice. You will know when to seek expert help and what your tax advisor will want to know during the year to help you.

WEALTH OPPORTUNITY: 401(K) PLANS

In 1980, a benefits consultant named Ted Benna found something in the tax rules that revolutionized retirement planning in the United States. Section 401(k) of the Internal Revenue Code allowed employees to shelter income from tax by deferring its receipt to a later date. Benna convinced the IRS to go beyond this and allow employees to establish separate accounts funded by the sheltered income.

From that beginning arose the ubiquitous 401(k). Companies design the plans, and employees manage their own accounts. Tens of millions of Americans have trillions of dollars of assets in these plans that provide employees covered by them access to a robust savings and investment platform.

An employee is allowed to shelter a portion of their income, up to a cap of $19,500 if they are under 50 and $26,000 if they are over 50. This annual limit is adjusted by the government for inflation. The account is invested, and the income and growth generated by those investments is tax-deferred, meaning you don't pay any tax on it while it is in the 401(k). At retirement (or earlier, subject to certain exceptions), withdrawals taken from the 401(k) are considered taxable income. This dual tax break—the annual income sheltering and the tax deferral—is a great deal. Given this tax break's power, the sooner you can take advantage of it, and the sooner you can contribute the maximum to your plan, the larger your lifetime benefit will be.

continued

Start early

Let's say you're a new 25-year-old employee and decide that you have other priorities besides contributing to your 401(k). Some may make sense, like paying off student loans or saving for a house, and some won't, like that retirement is for old people and you need money for cool things now. You're going to skip 401(k) contributions and make it up later with larger amounts—ten years later to be exact. Let's say at that point you contribute $10,000 and increase the contribution every year by 3 percent to account for inflation. Assume the 401(k) plan earns 8 percent per year. Thirty years later, at the age of sixty-five, your account will be worth $1,527,079. Not bad.

Now, look over to the next cubicle at the guy who started work the same day as you and decided that, even though he doesn't have much money, he would invest in his 401(k) from the beginning. He only contributes $5,000 that first year and increases it every year by the same 3 percent. He earns the same 8 percent as you do, but by the time he's sixty-five, he's had an extra ten years of compounding to help his cause. Despite the fact that over the years he has contributed $100,000 less into his account than you have into yours, it is worth $319,169 more than yours when you're both sixty-five.

Annual tax break

With 401(k) contributions, you're sheltering yourself from income tax. Assuming your marginal tax rate federally is 25 percent and you max out your 401(k) contribution at $19,500, you'll save $4,875 in taxes every year. Do that for thirty years (without assuming any return on the money saved on taxes but assuming your annual contribution goes up by inflation), and the tax savings would be more than $215,000.

Tax-deferred growth

Investing the inflation-adjusted annual contributions in a portfolio that earned 8 percent per year for thirty years would lead to $2,825,096. Assume you did that in a brokerage account (where the growth is subject to tax annually), instead of in a 401(k). If you lost 1 percent of that return per year to taxes, you'd have $427,037 less. Combine that with the tax savings above, and you're looking at a net difference of $639,788.

One percent is obviously an estimate, but it's reasonable. Long-term capital gains and dividends are taxed every year at 15 percent or 20 percent, depending on your tax bracket; short-term gains and nonmunicipal bond income are taxed at your ordinary rate. Therefore, if we estimate you'd lose 12 percent to taxes, that represents less than the tax rates assessed on portfolio earnings, which makes sense given that your portfolio will always have some deferred gains in it that are not realized.

Nay to the naysayers

The above analysis shows the 401(k) with $427,037 more than the brokerage account. Some would claim that this sum is overstated, because the 401(k) has never been taxed, and its distributions will be income you have to pay taxes on. Conversely, the brokerage account has been at least partially taxed along the way. Plus, the brokerage account, if it was all invested efficiently (in terms of taxes) in stocks, will likely only have dividends and long-term capital gains, which are taxed at lower rates than what people pay on the income that comes out of their 401(k).

Both of these are somewhat valid points, but don't overthink it. The government is giving you a huge break by saying you can shelter some of your annual income and defer the earnings on your portfolio for decades. It would take some creative modeling to prove that rejecting that offer would be a good idea.

Free money

Most employers will contribute some money for you to your 401(k) account. They do this typically by matching your contributions through various formulas, although some provide contributions without requiring employee contributions. The most common matches are 3 percent to 4 percent of your salary. Not contributing to the plan at the level needed to get the maximum match leaves free money on the table, and that free money skews the benefits even further toward saving in your 401(k).

Employers can and do contribute beyond the match through

continued

profit-sharing plans. These are often paired with 401(k) plans and allow companies to give their employees a share of profits annually in a contribution that is typically added to their 401(k) balance.

Using your 401(k)

Now comes the harder part: figuring out how to invest this money. Once you've chosen an investment strategy, 401(k) plans make it easier because they allow you to direct all future contributions to an investment mix you've selected. However, you still have to come up with that initial strategy.

The challenge is wading through the different investment options and choosing the best mix of funds for your situation.

The most common option is a target date fund, offered by mutual fund families as a simple one-stop investment solution. Although this type of fund is not limited to retirement plans, it is typically associated with them and prevalent on 401(k) investment menus. You simply choose a target date that is closest to your desired retirement year; the date will be right in the name of the fund. For example, the ACME Target Date 2045 fund would be the choice for someone who wanted to retire in 2045. The fund family then manages the target date fund with that year in mind. They create an asset allocation glide path that shifts the fund's allocation more conservatively as the target date approaches. A target date fund typically invests in many of the fund family's underlying mutual funds to implement its asset allocation. The glide path can be found online by investors interested in understanding the portfolio now and its intended evolution. Target date funds are popular because they are convenient, are easier to use and understand than other investment options, and eliminate the need for plan participants to actively manage their 401(k) accounts. You delegate account management to the fund family by selecting the right target date. There's a lot to like.

There are also some things not to like. The two biggest in my opinion are that the glide paths are predetermined and only factor the expected retirement date into the asset allocation. First, the current investment environment, and whether certain asset classes are expensive or attractive, are not part of the asset allocation decision. You are basically saying that you know in 2018 what you should be buying and selling every year until 2045. Second, the target retirement date may not mean as much as you think it does to your investment strategy. Let's say you are retiring in 2045. You might only be sixty years old, have sufficient assets invested elsewhere, and be able to delay making withdrawals from your retirement accounts until you are forced to through the required minimum distribution rules after you turn 72. Or your 401(k) could be your only large asset and you begin pulling money out right away. In that hypothetical situation, there is at least a ten-year difference in the time when withdrawals will be made that isn't factored into the glide path. Neither is the expected size of the withdrawals. Yes, retirement age is one important factor, but if you are going to withdraw 5.5 percent from your 401(k), as an example, and I am only going to need to withdraw 2 percent, shouldn't that percentage be factored into our asset allocation? Of course it should, but it can't with a target date fund.

I'm not sure how you can remedy the first issue with target date funds, and to a certain extent that's fine, since you have outsourced your account management to a target date provider and probably don't have the inclination, ability, or time to outguess the target date fund providers' asset allocation. The second issue can be partly remedied by being aware of it and choosing a target date that more realistically aligns with when you expect to withdraw from the fund. You may not know at a younger age, which is okay, because the fund will be growth-oriented for most of your time in it. As retirement gets closer and you do have more information, that is when it'll be important to choose the more precise target date.

Changing jobs

When you change jobs, you have options for what to do with your 401(k), so long as it has a large enough balance (typically above $5,000). If it's below that level, your old employer may require you to take a distribution out of the plan. Otherwise, you can determine whether you should roll the old account into your new company's plan, keep it where it is, or roll it into an IRA. Cashing it out and paying a penalty is obviously not one of the options we're going to consider, because the entire balance will be taxed and a further 10 percent penalty assessed.

continued

A rollover to an IRA will be a tax-free event, and the account balance can continue to grow tax-deferred. Furthermore, you can open your IRA somewhere where you have unlimited investment options, as opposed to the limited menu of an employer plan. It's usually your best bet.

However, if either your new employer or your old one has really strong 401(k) plans, you may choose to use one of those instead. By really strong, I mean they have a broad list of investment options that cover all of the asset classes you want to be invested in and at a low cost. If you do decide to roll it into your new employer's plan, understand that you've lost the option to roll it into an IRA with unlimited investment flexibility until you leave the new company. The benefits are that you may continue making backdoor Roth contributions through an empty traditional IRA and possibly have greater protections from creditors or lawsuits. There's one exception to this, known as an in-service withdrawal, but that's likely not available to you until your sixties.

Borrowing from your 401(k)

Finally, please don't borrow from your 401(k) plan. You're usually allowed to do so by your work plan, and it can be tempting, particularly if your other debt is high-interest and a lower-interest 401(k) loan would be more attractive. There are multiple reasons I don't recommend it.

First, you're spending money that was invested and growing tax-deferred. Some people try to soften the blow by saying that when you pay the loan back plus interest, you're paying yourself back. Well, the money you use to pay the loan back is after-tax money that then goes into the 401(k) and will be taxed again when you withdraw it after retirement. Also, if you don't make payments on it within ninety days, the loan amount is considered a distribution that will be taxed and penalized. Finally, if you change jobs, the loan needs to be paid off within sixty days to avoid taxes and penalties. It's not worth it.

PART 2

Capital Allocation

"In the long run, it's not just how much money you make that will determine your future prosperity. It's how much of that money you put to work by saving it and investing it."

—Peter Lynch

Making quality long-term investments to prime that compounding machine moves us on to the allocation portion of capital allocation. Working with debt and cash, investing in a traditional portfolio of stocks and bonds (either by yourself or through an advisor), using real estate as an investment stream, and when to consider other investment types are crucial skills for allocating your capital for maximum gains. But first of all, you need to understand one simple fact:

YOU CAN'T SAVE YOUR WAY TO
FINANCIAL INDEPENDENCE

Learning that you can't save your way to financial independence is important for two reasons. First, having enough money to retire comfortably, become wealthy, or be financially independent is not easy and requires skill and planning. We need the capital you've allocated to grow faster than it would in your bank account or certificate of deposit (CD) for you to hit a long-term goal such as retirement.

YOU MUST PLAN FOR A LONG RETIREMENT

Your retirement will likely last decades, so plan accordingly. According to data from the Social Security Administration, men who reach the age of sixty-five have a life expectancy of 84.3 years, and women reaching that age have a life expectancy of 86.7 years. A quarter of all sixty-five-year-olds live to ninety, and 10 percent of them live to ninety-five. And, as we can see from the chart below, the affluent live even longer. A prudent ending point is ninety-five. That means funding at least a thirty-year retirement—longer if you retire earlier and shorter if you retire later.

YOU NEED A LOT OF MONEY TO
RETIRE COMFORTABLY

Your specific retirement nest egg target depends on your situation and can't be determined through a general rule found online or in financial planning books. For a more accurate number, you should build a retirement budget influenced by your current spending; your future spending reductions, like a mortgage getting paid off or less support for your kids as they leave home; and future spending

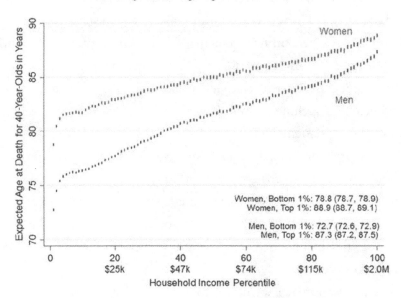

Life Expectancy By Income Level

Women

Men

Women, Bottom 1%: 78.8 (78.7, 78.9)
Women, Top 1%: 88.9 (88.7, 89.1)

Men, Bottom 1%: 72.7 (72.6, 72.9)
Men, Top 1%: 87.3 (87.2, 87.5)

Expected Age at Death for 40-Year-Olds in Years

| 0 | 20 | 40 | 60 | 80 | 100 |
| | $25k | $47k | $74k | $115k | $2.0M |

Household Income Percentile

increases, like travel and health care. However, shortcuts can give us estimated savings targets.

A first approach would be to target a specific sum of money, like $2 million. It seems reasonable and the simplicity is appealing. The problem is that it may or may not be enough, depending on how much you'll spend each year of your estimated thirty-two-year retirement. Let's assume your retirement portfolio earns 6 percent per year after fees and taxes. If you needed to withdraw 7 percent per year, equal to $140,000 in the first year, your assets would last thirty-seven years—longer than target retirement length. But at a higher spending need, like $200,000 in that first retirement year, your withdrawal rate will only afford a sixteen-year retirement—half of what you need. A planning guideline that leaves you broke halfway through retirement stinks.

A second option would be to target saving enough to replace a percentage of your current income—say, 80 percent. If your income is $250,000, you would target an annual retirement spending need of $200,000 (80 percent replacement). We'll assume you would spend 3 percent more each year to keep up with inflation. Again, your retirement is thirty-two years, and you're earning 6 percent after fees and taxes. Crunching the numbers shows you'll need $4,006,479 to fund this retirement.

You probably already know my issue with this: The number should be based on what you'll spend in retirement, not what you're making now. What if you have a high savings rate while working (which you obviously will now that you've read part 1)? The portion of your income dedicated to savings clearly doesn't need to be replaced in retirement.

A third approach would be to save a multiple of your current income. Let's use eleven for this example. Using $250,000 again for your current income times eleven equals $2,750,000.

You'll notice that we arrived at three very different estimates with our three strategies. And the kicker is that none of these may work for you; they're just too general. You need to estimate what you'll actually spend during your thirty-two years of retirement and plan for that goal, not some nebulous guideline that might over- or undershoot your needs.

YOU NEED TO EARN STRONG RETURNS TO HAVE ENOUGH MONEY

Occasionally, advisors get asked a good but basic question: Why should you invest? After all, investing entails risks—some real, like permanently losing money, and some imagined, like portfolio volatility. Wouldn't you be better off just putting your money in a CD or savings account to avoid those risks?

There are pages and pages and book after book that can be written to address all of the underlying themes and questions in that dialogue. Fortunately for you, we're going to narrow it down and focus on the aspect relevant to this section. You need to invest because most of us can't save enough to fund a future goal like retirement without having our savings grow.

Here's where those hypothetical savings targets come back in. By sixty-three, you need savings of $2 million, $2.75 million, or $4 million, according to our overly general calculations. Let's say you start saving in earnest at thirty-three and that your cash, CD, or government bond returns are 2.5 percent after fees and taxes.

For $2 million, you will need to save $45,555 per year. That's not impossible but would be damn hard. Remember: This is your lowest retirement hurdle. Using our 6 percent investment growth rate, you would need to save a much more manageable $25,298 per year—just over half the estimate without that 6 percent growth. The two savings targets for $2.75 million are $62,639 with a 2.5 percent return and $34,785 with a 6 percent return. For $4 million, they are $91,111 at a 2.5 percent return and $50,596 at 6 percent. In this last instance, you have to save $40,515 less at 6 percent than at 2.5 percent. With all three retirement targets, you have half the savings burden just by investing.

Retirement based only on saving money—without investment— simply isn't an option for most of us. Most of us can't just save our way to long-term goals like retirement or financial independence. Retirement will last decades, we'll need a lot of money to do it comfortably, and it'll be much easier to do if our money earns decent returns. That's one important reason why we're focusing on allocating capital in part 2 of this book.

YOU'RE ON YOUR OWN

In the past, more US employers helped fund employee retirements through pension plans. This defined benefit was often a retirement annuity that historically provided a large percentage of retirement income. For many reasons not relevant here, pension plans are less common now, having been replaced by defined contribution plans, like 401(k)s, which rely primarily on employee contributions and investment.

We need to be capital allocators now more than ever, but are we well equipped to do it? How many of us took personal finance classes in high school or college that prepared us to manage money? Do we understand the investment options in our 401(k) plans and feel comfortable making strong choices between them? Do we understand how the tax code works, and could we review our tax returns to find missed planning opportunities?

Most of us do not and cannot. The skills that allowed you to generate and save capital are not the same ones needed to effectively grow capital. Said differently, your job and career skills don't provide much help with growing money.

Career success is only the start, and it leaves you ill-equipped for the remaining journey. That's a problem, and the more successful you are, the more capital you have, and the more essential it will be to possess a framework for allocating it. Successful capital allocators spend a significant amount of time trying to make smart decisions and improving their skills. They prioritize wealth accumulation activities: learning, investing, meeting with professional advisors, budgeting, tracking expenses, and so on—and you must do the same.

	1998	1999	2000	2001	2002	2003	2004	2005	2006	2007	2008	2009	2010	2011	2012	2013
Total DB plans	299	296	294	290	285	277	263	242	224	202	185	171	151	139	123	118
Traditional DB plans	251	236	228	206	187	169	157	138	125	105	88	75	57	48	39	34
Hybrid DB plans	48	60	66	84	98	108	106	104	99	97	97	96	94	91	84	84
DC plan only	195	200	202	206	212	220	234	256	275	297	315	329	349	361	377	382

Change in usage of defined benefit and defined contribution plans 1998–2013

Notes: Sponsorship shows as type of plan offered to salaried new hires at year-end. Trend data are shown for the 2013 Fortune 500 companies and capture changes to their retirement plans from 1998 through 2013.

* Sums do not equal 500 because a small number of the 2013 Fortune 500 companies did not exist in earlier years.

Source: Towers Watson analysis of 2013 Fortune 500

CHAPTER 4

What to Do with Cash, Debt, and Bad Investments

"A company is generally focused on gaining profits . . . One would think, then, that when it comes to money, companies would tend to know what they are doing, which is one reason it's important for wealthy individuals and families to explore thinking and acting the way that companies do."

—Thomas J. Anderson

B usinesses exist to make their owners money by allocating capital effectively. They deploy their cash received from operations, borrowing, or selling stock to make money by reinvesting in their business, buying companies or other productive assets, purchasing their own shares, retiring debt, or paying dividends. Each path has its advantages, and strong corporate capital allocators decide between them.

Individuals benefit from tailoring this corporate framework for personal use since corporate finance is a well-developed field with trillions of dollars riding on its effectiveness. Key concepts have been distilled that can be translated for individuals looking to apply a disciplined approach to building their wealth.

Corporations have the following sources of capital: the cash they receive from their business operations, borrowed money, issuing shares in the company, and selling assets. Individuals have a shorter list: their savings, borrowed money, and assets that can be sold (otherwise known as divestment).

Debt and divestment are more complicated, so we will discuss those two capital sources and how to incorporate them into your allocation plan in a second. But first, let's dispense with one last financial planning basic related to your capital and make sure you have it covered before making long-term investments.

CASH

A rainy day fund protects you from having to go into debt or sell long-term investments at a loss to cover emergency expenses. It's the first thing you should save for, and only once it's done should you move on to other things.

The Certified Financial Planner Board of Standards recommends maintaining three to six months of living expenses in cash, depending on your situation and the economic climate. Target a larger cushion if your income is volatile, if you have less job security, or if you have larger financial obligations.

People can overdo how much cash they set aside, particularly once they have nonretirement accounts invested in a mix of stocks and bonds, but being a bit cash heavy won't harm you so long as you aren't setting too much aside simply so you can spend it.

DEBT

Debt is an important tool for any capital allocator. It's also a complicated one. Debt means borrowing money and paying interest. For some, that's not an issue, while others have an emotional or even a spiritual aversion to it. Emotions complicate investing. Debt can enhance returns, which we'll get to shortly, but it comes with greater risk, as it can multiply your losses and wipe you out. Combining your emotions with the math gives you a source of capital that is misunderstood, underused, and overused all at the same time. My goal is to help you strip out the emotion and find the right amount of debt to use in your capital allocation plan.

Leverage (using debt to purchase additional assets) can increase returns. A $10,000 investment that earns 10 percent generates $1,000. Ten thousand dollars used as collateral to borrow another $10,000 in the same investment generates $2,000 minus the borrowing cost.

Leverage also magnifies losses. Borrowing $10,000 and investing in something that loses 100 percent leaves you broke. Borrowing $10,000 off of the initial $10,000 and losing it all leaves you $10,000 in debt. Leverage magnifies weak performance exactly when you don't want it magnified.

Leverage is addictive. Once they get the bug, few people revert to more conservative practices. But as we all learned in 2008, when a loss hits, it doesn't care how good you thought the investment was. History is full of smart people who detonate their financial life through leverage addictions. Read *The Quants* and *When Genius Failed*, two fantastic books about investment "geniuses" who blew up this way.

That doesn't mean you should eschew debt. Strong capital allocators don't ignore tools. You need to borrow when it makes strong financial sense to do so, meaning the opportunities to profit from borrowing are powerful or the borrowing costs are low. Learn when and how to do this analysis for yourself. Be careful, not fearful.

BORROW FOR PROTECTION

Borrow for protection, not just to capitalize on opportunities. In 2006, Ford Motor Company's then CEO, Alan Mulally, made a capital allocation decision regarding debt that's been called Ford's salvation and one of the most significant moves in the company's 105-year history.[12] When borrowing was easy, Mulally mortgaged the company's assets, including the Mustang brand name and Ford logo, for $23.6 billion in loans to finance a company overhaul and to give Ford "a cushion to protect for a recession or other unexpected event."[13] We now know that a severe recession came soon after. Car sales plummeted. General Motors and Chrysler, Ford's domestic competitors, sought bankruptcy protection and received billions of dollars in a controversial government bailout. Ford did not have to do either of these things thanks to its cash hoard. It emerged from the crisis stronger, which helped its image, reputation, and stock price.

---

12   Bill Vlasic, "Choosing Its Own Path, Ford Stayed Independent," *The New York Times*, April 9, 2009, https://dealbook.nytimes.com/2009/04/09/choosing-its-own-path-ford-stayed-independent/.

13   Vlasic, "Ford Stayed Independent."

Individuals can do something similar by setting up lines of credit when times are good in case they're needed for bad times. One of the most common sources of credit lines available to individuals is a home equity line of credit (HELOC), which allows you to borrow against your home equity. Once it has been established, you can borrow up to the limit or never tap into it at all. There's a draw period of ten years, after which you enter a repayment period for up to twenty years, although you can always make payments against the line during the draw period.

Most HELOC lenders lend up to 85 percent of your home equity. For example, if your home is worth $500,000 and you have a $250,000 mortgage on it, your equity is $250,000, and 85 percent of that is $212,500. Besides your home equity, the lender evaluates your credit score and history, work history, income, and current debt.

HELOC rates are variable, meaning that, as interest rates increase or decrease, the loan rate moves accordingly. It is based on some standard index like the US prime rate plus whatever margin the lender adds. Rates vary widely, so it's important to shop around. Some lenders offer introductory rates. Check the fine print to see what those rates will adjust to after the honeymoon period.

BORROWING TO MAKE MONEY

Debt is a source of capital for investing, but you need to decide the right debt levels for your capital allocation plan. It'll be less than the maximum amount of debt you can borrow. Adding debt increases risk to a company and its shareholders, and it does the same to an individual. Yes, it can be profitable, but you need to exercise caution, ensure the debt is worth the risk, and borrow safely.

Corporate capital allocators can rely on established corporate finance best practices to determine optimal debt levels for their situation. Those corporate debt ratios are determined on the basis of how stable the company's cash flow is, what return they are targeting with the debt, and how tolerant the management and owners are of borrowing. Individuals can use a similar framework to guide their own borrowing decisions.

In *The Value of Debt*, Thomas J. Anderson suggests that, based on applying the principles of corporate debt management to individuals, the optimal debt ratio for a wealthy individual is around 25 percent, usually ranging from 15 percent to 35 percent. The debt ratio is calculated by dividing your total debt by your net worth.

For example, assume that you have the following assets and liabilities:

Assets	Liabilities
Savings and investment accounts of $1 million	Mortgage of $400,000
Retirement accounts of $500,000	
Home worth $600,000	
Total assets	$2,100,000 million
Total liabilities	$400,000
Debt ratio	19% ($400,000/$2,100,000)

That range of 15 percent to 35 percent is a helpful target but also a wide one. Anderson recommends working with a financial advisor to personalize a target for yourself based on your situation, similar to how a corporation would do it. The factors below can facilitate that conversation.

Factor 1: Stability and strength of cash flow

Rarely do smart individuals get loans they can't pay principal and interest on with their current income. The main way debt becomes a serious problem is when one's income unexpectedly drops, but those monthly payments still need to be made. It's therefore logical to assess the stability of your cash flow. The more consistent cash flow you have, the more you can borrow, because covering the payments will not be a challenge.

High job security and strong income make it easier to borrow. A lower-paying job, variable pay, and less job security should lead to less borrowing. Stress test your cash flow and compare it to your total debt payments to make sure you can maintain your standard of living and make your debt payments if your income drops. Factor these debt payments into how much cash you're targeting as a rainy day fund. If your income were interrupted for six to twelve months, could you continue to make the debt payments?

Factor 2: Expected returns

The amount you borrow for an investment should be related to the returns you reasonably expect to make on the assets it's financing. You should only borrow to pursue attractive returns that easily exceed the cost of the borrowed funds. To be clear, what you expect to make on a project you're borrowing money for shouldn't change the maximum amount you can safely borrow. It's a maximum for a reason. The path to bankruptcy is paved with people who borrowed too much to invest in great ideas.

You have limited borrowing capacity. Don't waste it chasing low returns. Your opportunity cost is what you could have done with the debt instead. The return hurdle for borrowing isn't today's low rates but whether the returns are attractive enough compared to other investments. And please don't borrow to chase negative returns, meaning to spend, unless you're doing so for an essential purpose, like a home or a car, at a low enough rate that it's smarter to borrow and leave your money invested.

Factor 3: Personal preference

Your personal preference matters. Debt is a tool. Used correctly, it can make you money. Used poorly, it can wipe you out. Good capital allocators are open-minded and opportunistic. They don't shut the door on any tool, but they also don't fall blindly in love with any. I'd love for you to be the same way, but I also know that some people are uncomfortable borrowing money, may have a religious objection to it, or just can't sleep at night when in debt. We're trying to make you wealthy, not miserable. We're also trying to create strategies you can stick to. Something you enter into reluctantly is probably not something you'll commit to over the long term. And you need to be able to commit. It's rare for an investment idea to immediately pay off, so you'll have those loans for a while.

MARGIN LOANS

Margin loans, or borrowing against your taxable portfolio, are similar to a HELOC; your brokerage firm will allow you to borrow using your investments as collateral. This cannot be done with retirement accounts, since to borrow against retirement accounts causes them to lose their tax-advantaged status. Like other debt sources, margin should be used carefully since it can put your portfolio at risk for large losses. However, within reasonable limits, it should be another tool in your capital allocation kit.

A margin loan is an adjustable rate loan. *The Value of Debt* summarizes its advantages: no expenses or costs when you don't use it, no prepayment penalties, no credit fees, no application fees, no underwriting, and the loans aren't reported to the credit bureaus. You also don't have to make any scheduled payments against interest or principal. The first considered use of it should be as a line of credit, similar to a home equity line. In the event you need short-term funds, you can temporarily withdraw them on margin and pay it back later.

You can also invest on margin. You're typically allowed to borrow up to 50 percent of your portfolio value, although you need to be well below that threshold to avoid a margin call, which can happen if your portfolio equity falls below a certain threshold—typically, 25 percent to 40 percent; let's use 33 percent here. If you have a $1 million portfolio and borrow $500,000 to purchase more investments, you have portfolio equity of $1,500,000 and a $500,000 loan— exactly 33 percent of your equity. If the portfolio value decreases so that you fall below the 33 percent line, you will have to sell securities at a loss to pay down the loan or add cash to the account—two negative outcomes we won't risk. Let's say that, instead of the $500,000 loan, you borrow $200,000. Your equity is now $1.2 million. Your margin is $200,000. The investments would have to decrease by 50 percent for you to have a margin call. It's possible to have a 50 percent loss but much more difficult, particularly if you don't concentrate your portfolio and diversify it beyond stocks.

You can also use margin to make investments outside your portfolio. This won't increase your portfolio equity, so the math is different. For example, in the $200,000 loan scenario, you have borrowed 20 percent of the equity in the portfolio. A portfolio loss of 40 percent to $600,000 would put you at the 33 percent maintenance requirement—too close for comfort. You'll need to borrow less if you are investing outside of your portfolio.

All debt decisions are difficult, because debt provides potential advantages that can easily become concrete disadvantages. Understand the pros and cons, evaluate based on the current environment and opportunity, borrow limited amounts, and consider worst-case scenarios.

DIVESTMENT

A final source of capital is money tied up in a poor investment or project. Investment geeks call this divestment. Scrutinize the return expectations of your current investments to make sure you're not committing capital to weak ideas. Capital is a precious commodity that shouldn't be wasted chasing low returns.

Companies shed underperforming assets to free up capital to earn higher returns. Individuals should do the same. I take my clients with multiple projects or investments through an analysis of return expectations and risks and decide if anything they own is locking up capital in an underperforming asset. Do they have a rental property that isn't a great investment or a vacation home that's bleeding cash? Should they sell a piece of land they were hoping to develop or get out of a private investment that's just not doing well? The freed-up capital can be deployed elsewhere.

CREATE YOUR ROAD MAP

Individuals have fewer sources of capital than corporations do— three, to be precise: savings, debt, and divestment. However, there is still a wealth of knowledge about how companies use their capital that can help individuals create their own strategies and road map.

Look at your financial obligations, how much you make, and how stable your pay is, and set aside a rainy day fund in cash, in a money market account, or in high-quality short-term bonds to protect your long-term investment plan from having to be derailed by a financial emergency. Seek a greater rainy day cushion by opening lines of credit, like a HELOC and margin loans, when times are good. Carry over some of that analysis to figure out how much debt you want to use in your capital allocation plan. A general recommendation based on a review of corporate finance is 15 percent to 35 percent of your net worth. Use the factors of cash-flow stability, return expectations, and personal preference to reach your own target. Finally, assess your current projects and investments to see if the capital you have tied up in them can be put to better use.

CHAPTER 5

Starting to Invest

"In the real world, you uncover an opportunity, and then you compare other opportunities with that. And you only invest in the most attractive opportunities. That's your opportunity cost . . . It's your alternatives that matter."

—Charlie Munger[14]

We need to define opportunity cost and how to apply it using return hurdles—target returns to be aware of when comparing investment opportunities—as Charlie Munger's quote above recommends. Since those return hurdles center around

---

14   Tren Griffin, "A Dozen Things I've Learned from Charlie Munger About Capital Allocation," 25iq.com, October 3, 2015, https://25iq.com/2015/10/03/a-dozen-things-ive-learned-from-charlie-munger-about-capital-allocation.

potential traditional stock and bond portfolios, we'll highlight different estimation methods for those future returns.

OPPORTUNITY COST AND RETURN HURDLES

We've danced around opportunity cost at least twice so far, and it's now time for a deeper dive. Opportunity cost is what you give up when choosing one thing over another. It's a simple formula. Your investment returns 5 percent, but one you missed returns 10 percent, leaving your opportunity cost as 5 percent. Since you have limited capital and must maximize that capital's growth, you can't commit to weaker investments that prevent investing in more attractive ones. The opportunity cost won't show up on a spreadsheet anywhere, but it's real, and we need to guard against it. We need to learn what an attractive return is so we can either make or pass on an investment.

Comparing investments can get technical, forcing you to bust out your financial calculator or an Excel spreadsheet. Good investors evaluate what future cash they will receive from an investment, discount those cash flows (a fancy way of saying they try to determine what the cash is worth today), and use that number to value the investment and compare it to other opportunities. You can learn how to do this, but at the risk of being simplistic, I don't think you need to.

Rather than running multiple discounted cash-flow models whose results will be highly sensitive to their assumptions, we can center our return hurdles on traditional stock and bond portfolios. While this is also not a perfect approach, there are multiple reasons to do so: There is a long return history with these investments. Stock and bond returns are your most accessible investment returns; I call them hassle-free. Plunk some money into your 401(k) or brokerage account, buy a diversified stock mutual fund or balanced fund, and twenty years later, you'll probably be happy. Hassle-free doesn't mean easy, guaranteed, or stress-free, but it does mean the most accessible.

Since they're the most accessible, it makes sense to use them as a starting point, since nontraditional investments that require more work should target higher returns. While it's true that the current investment and economic climate can cause future returns to deviate from history, there are ways to factor that into your return expectations.

TRADITIONAL MARKET RETURNS

We've determined that we're going to use stock and bond returns to make opportunity cost comparisons. Let's now look at three methods for establishing traditional portfolio expected returns. The first is history, the second is third-party return expectations, and the third is commonly accepted formulas to calculate your own.

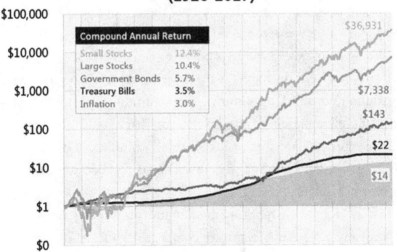

Ibbotson SBBI Stocks, Bonds, Bills, and Inflation (1926-2017)

Compound Annual Return	
Small Stocks	12.4%
Large Stocks	10.4%
Government Bonds	5.7%
Treasury Bills	3.5%
Inflation	3.0%

Source: Ibbotson

HISTORIC RETURNS

The table above shows that, historically, stocks have returned between 10.4 percent (large company or large cap stocks) and 12.4 percent (small company or small cap stocks) per year. The average between them is 11.4 percent, but since people don't typically hold half their portfolio in small company stocks, let's shortcut this a bit and use the large cap return history of 10 percent.

Risk-free T-bills have returned between 3.5 percent and Treasury bonds have returned 5.7 percent. The average between them is 4.6 percent. T-bills are short-term debt issued at a discount by the US Treasury with a maturity of less than one year. Treasury bonds are longer-term debt issued with a fixed interest rate by the US Treasury.

There are other types of bonds to consider, like high-quality corporate bonds issued by corporations with strong credit ratings, municipal bonds issued by states and municipalities, and high-yield corporate bonds issued by corporations with weaker credit ratings. Their return histories are different, but government bonds work well for a return hurdle exercise. They provide a safe and reliable starting point, and you can always incorporate those other bonds into your portfolio if it makes sense to do so.

Using history as a guide, stocks are at 10 percent, and bonds are at 4.6 percent. It doesn't make sense to use a 100 percent bond portfolio to establish opportunity cost return hurdles, since government bonds represent a safe investment that should not generate strong returns. Therefore, using them as a hurdle could cause you to be attracted to unimpressive investments just because they beat government bonds.

I'd be fine with ignoring bonds and only using stocks, but it's reasonable to not want to compare all future investments against a 100 percent stock portfolio that will experience plenty of short-term volatility while racking up impressive long-term returns. So let's use the ubiquitous 60/40 portfolio, often touted as a great basic asset allocation for a growth-oriented investor who wants some diversification and downside protection: 60 percent stocks and 40 percent bonds. The historical average return for that portfolio is 7.8 percent.

This leaves us with two historical return hurdles we can use: 10 percent per year if we're looking only at 100 percent stocks and 7.8 percent if we incorporate bonds.

THIRD PARTIES

Certain groups publish annual capital market assumptions, or what they expect future investment returns to be, that can provide a viable alternative to history for setting target returns. A strong example of one such survey is put out by Horizon Actuarial Services. Horizon is an actuarial firm for large pension plans in the United States. Actuaries need realistic return assumptions for the pension plan work they do. Since 2010, Horizon has asked various investment advisors what their risk and return expectations are for different asset classes and averaged their answers in their annual report. The 2018 report involved thirty-four surveyed firms and is available as a free PDF through the Horizon website at horizonactuarial.com.

The report provides return expectations for sixteen different asset classes, plus inflation. It breaks stocks out to include developed international countries and emerging markets. It also includes multiple categories of bonds and alternative investments like real estate and commodities. We're focused on just stocks and bonds, since those are our hurdle components. The 2018 results placed the average long-term (twenty-year) return for stocks at 7.8 percent. The government bond expected returns were 3.05 percent, and that gives us 5.9 percent for the 60/40 portfolio.

YOUR OWN RETURN EXPECTATIONS

The third method of establishing return hurdles is as much an investment lesson as anything else. In learning how to create your own projections, you will get a much better understanding of where investment returns come from. I hope this will also help you see why stock market volatility is ultimately best ignored, since reacting to it will interrupt your ability to make money.

It can be difficult to see how you actually make money with stocks. Many of us own them indirectly through mutual funds or exchange-traded funds (ETFs) that require some digging to uncover which stocks we actually own. Whether we own the stocks directly or through those vehicles, we tend to see the money we make (or lose) expressed in the price difference between what we paid for the investment and what we sold it for. A notable exception to this is dividend payments. Stocks or funds that pay dividends provide a direct and visible return, which connects to our main point. A stock is not a piece of paper or an electronic bookkeeping entry. It represents business ownership. A mutual fund and ETF represent ownership of multiple businesses. Your long-term gains will equal the long-term gains of those businesses.

In *The Little Book of Common Sense Investing*, investment legend Jack Bogle explains that stock market returns have two components: the investor return, which is our focus, and the speculative return (based on investors' speculations and shifting optimistic or pessimistic moods), which we should ignore. The investor return represents the underlying businesses' performance, and the speculative return is basically market movement, or how much investors are willing to pay for the business returns we have identified so far. If investors are optimistic and greedy, they'll pay higher multiples of the company's earnings, or more than they usually would for the same dollar of business earnings. If investors are pessimistic and fearful, they'll pay less for the same dollar of earnings. That fluctuation causes market prices for stocks to move in the short term much more than the performance of the underlying businesses represented by those stocks. That fluctuation can also trick investors into selling a good basket of businesses at a bad time.

Bogle defines investor return as the starting dividend yield plus subsequent annual earnings growth. I'll explain those terms next, but it's an approach to identify what your future cash flows will be by owning those businesses for the long term. A dividend is the amount of money a company pays its shareholders out of its profits or retained cash. The dividend yield of a stock equals the total dividends paid out per year divided by the stock price. If Acme Corp. paid a $0.25 quarterly dividend and had a share price of $25, its dividend yield would be 4 percent ($0.25 times 4, divided by $25). It's also possible to calculate the dividend yield of an entire market, like the S&P 500, so you can see what yield you'd receive annually for every dollar invested in that index.

Earnings are profits, or the money remaining after the company's expenses, and earnings growth is the percentage by which companies grow their earnings annually. The market has historically experienced 4 percent to 5 percent earnings growth. However, for Bogle's formula, we need an estimate of future earnings growth. If you have some way of projecting a deviation from history, fine. Otherwise, let's use 4 percent. Combined with our 1.8 percent yield from chapter 3, our stock market return expectations are 5.8 percent.

Let's turn to bonds, an easier exercise. Bonds historically have performed quite closely to their yield when purchased. Bogle uses a blend of 10-year Treasury bonds, which were yielding 3.2 percent in 2018, and investment-grade corporate bonds, which were yielding 4.25 percent in 2018. Using those gets you to a 10-year bond return expectation of 3.75 percent.

So our 100 percent stock portfolio with this third method has a 5.8 percent return expectation, and our 60/40 portfolio has a 4.98 percent return expectation. You're probably thinking that this great dissertation on return expectation has led to three very different answers and not enough workable advice. That's a fair point. But there are pros and cons to each approach that I want you to learn about and understand. Let's go through those now, and I'll end with a recommendation.

THE PROS AND CONS OF USING HISTORY

Historical returns are a reasonable proxy for future expected returns. Yes, we've all seen the disclaimer *Past performance is no guarantee of future results*, and it's true that history won't necessarily repeat itself. But historical returns dating back to the late 1920s provide a robust enough data set to tell you something about future market performance. It's not a cherry-picked short time period. Those ninety years have seen all kinds of economic and market environments that should feed into an informative long-term average.

So why even consider alternatives to a historical estimate? First, there has been a wide variation in historical returns. The S&P 500 has had ten-year average returns as low as minus 5 percent per year and higher than 20 percent per year. That massive spread shows the limitations of this approach. As usual, Warren Buffett probably said it best: "If past history was all that is needed to play the game of money, the richest people would be librarians."[15]

Second, simply put, price matters. The price you pay for an investment influences your long-term returns. The cheaper the better, so the people who don't use history think it's smarter to adjust your future expectations based on how expensive or cheap the market is at your starting point.

The chart below helps illustrate this point. You see the same variability with bonds. Long-term averages are just that—averages and not guarantees.

Valuations Drive Returns

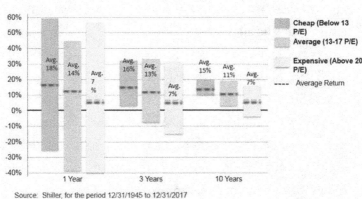

Used by permission of RegentAtlantic Capital[16]

---

15 Karl Kaufman, "Happy Birthday, Warren Buffett! Here are 30 of his best quotes," *Forbes*, August 30, 2018, https://www.forbes.com/sites/karlkaufman/2018/08/30/happy-birthday-warren-buffett-here-are-30-of-his-best-quotes/#4310e00e741e.

16 Andy Kapyrin, "How High for the Stock Market?," Regent Atlantic, January 17, 2018, https://regentatlantic.com/blog/high-high-stock-market/.

THE PROS AND CONS OF USING FORECASTS

This section applies both to using third-party return expectations and to creating your own, since, in both, you're deviating from history and forecasting an alternative. History is a good but flawed guide. Perhaps it can be improved on through a thoughtful forecast. We've already seen that starting price matters, and that's just one enhancement. Others exist, and smart people are constantly trying to determine where markets are headed. The investment holy grail of forecasting. Shouldn't we try it?

To quote Buffett again, "We've long felt that the only value of stock forecasters is to make fortune tellers look good."[17] Ouch. That's a bit harsh. It's also taken out of context; Buffett said it to caution against short-term market forecasting. Everyone makes long-term forecasts, whether they call them that or not—even Buffett. Deciding to invest money anywhere is a forecast that it'll earn a better return than the alternatives. But Buffett is spot on about short-term moves and market timing, which we will get into in the next chapter.

What about longer-term forecasts? They're better but still have issues. Simply put, they haven't worked. Research shows the unpredictability of returns, no matter the methodology or approach. This is key, because in choosing a return hurdle methodology, we're deciding whether long-term market returns will mirror history and, if they won't, whether we can predict the deviation.

Since we can't predict that deviation, there is a danger that ignoring history will hurt you financially. This is not just an exercise in theory. An example coming out of the recent credit crisis helps illustrate the point: Starting in November 2007, the US stock market tumbled into a bear market the likes of which most of us have never seen—a 57 percent decline over eighteen months. Scary stuff. A $100,000 portfolio

---

17   Berkshire Hathaway Corporation, *Annual Report 1992*, retrieved from https://www.berkshirehathaway.com/letters/letters.html.

of US stocks became $43,000, plus maybe a couple of thousand in dividend payments. Other markets tanked too. International markets, real estate, and commodities all got obliterated.

By March 2009, the market had bottomed, and although no one signaled the all clear, things had stopped declining. By the summer, many money managers were salivating over how cheap things had become. It was time to shop for stocks at bargain basement prices and watch them recover.

Only not so, according to one prominent investment manager with a different forecast. Bill Gross is a former portfolio manager at the Janus Capital Group who also cofounded the world's largest global bond fund manager, Pimco. Known as the Bond King, he ran that company's flagship strategy for years, was named fund manager of the decade by Morningstar, and was a three-time winner of its fixed-income manager of the year award. He told investors to stay away. In speeches and print, Gross warned that the brutal bear market that had just finished would not lead to great returns. We were in a "new normal," where stocks would earn very little compared to their long-term averages. Investors needed to recalibrate their long-term expectations because of our permanently downgraded economy and other such blather and blunder.

Well, then. We could have listened to the Bond King. It would have been easy to do. Who wants to dive into investments that can lose more than half their value in a year and a half? Who wants to do it before it's crystal clear that things have recovered? Not many. It's easy to rely on a brilliant slogan backed up by intelligent-sounding rhetoric and keep safe. But how would we have done if we'd followed that advice? Exactly nine years later, listening to slogans would have cost you the opportunity to triple your money—as in three times your initial investment, 13 percent annual returns. That's way better than the long-term averages—30 percent per year better.

Do I sound annoyed? Don't worry; I am. Nonsense like this (and Gross wasn't the only one, by far) helped keep investors out of this market for way too long. Indeed, some never got back in. Following forecasts has real-world implications. If you followed this one, you missed an unbelievable period of returns. That's one of the great cons of using forecasted returns.

WHAT SHOULD YOU DO INSTEAD?

So here's that concrete advice I promised you: Start with history but take a haircut to it to be conservative. Instead of 10 percent returns for stocks, 4.45 percent for bonds, and 8 percent for the blended portfolio, let's use 9 percent for stocks and 3 percent for bonds, giving the blended portfolio a 6.6 percent return. If 9 percent strikes you as too optimistic for the next twenty years, go to 8.5 percent. Anything beyond that and you're going to have to let me know what type of modeling you're doing that's convinced you that for the next twenty years stocks will return over 15 percent less than their long-term average.

In this chapter, we started with the opportunity cost to give us a sense of what return to target when making an investment. Since stocks and bonds provide accessible returns and a long performance history, we anchored our return hurdles to them. We then discussed different ways to create return expectations for them, including using history, following credible third-party long-term forecasts, and creating your own. In the end, history is a great guide but not conservative enough, and forecasting is iffy and sometimes overly conservative. Better to start with history and chop it down from there.

CHAPTER 6

Working with an Advisor

"You get recessions, you have stock market declines. If you don't understand that's going to happen, then you're not ready; you won't do well in the markets."

—Peter Lynch

There are three main reasons it makes sense to work with the right professional advisor: With a professional to share knowledge with you, you do not need to master investing to grow your net worth. Investing is competitive, and you need an edge to succeed; an advisor brings that edge. Emotions somehow always knock individual investors from their long-term plan, and the professional distance of an advisor—between you and your investments—can shield you from catastrophe.

That said, finding the right advisor can be difficult, but if you follow some simple guidelines and do your homework, you'll be able to narrow the field quickly.

MASTERY ISN'T ESSENTIAL

Personal finance books tend to fall into one of two camps: financial planning basics or how to invest like the pros. What if you know the basics already and aren't interested in picking and monitoring your own investments? This is fine, and likely preferable, since it's goofy to imagine you can master a professional task like investing in your spare time. Focusing on investing also leaves you without enough knowledge about capital allocation, which is the more essential skill. Traditional investing is only a tool in the capital allocation kit. It can be outsourced. Capital allocation, which is basically effective decision-making with your assets, cannot.

Hiring an advisor is how you outsource traditional investing. Your advisor brings their professional training and years of experience—education you don't have to build for yourself. Pro advisors have contacts and access to tools that help them evaluate investments better than an amateur can. Combine that with their experience, and you have a crucial advantage over going it alone. Advisors also offer group investments. As I've mentioned before, making money is easier when you already have money. By pooling your money with others', your advisor allows you and everyone else in the group to grow their capital exponentially faster. Finally, your advisor invests for a living. They're not trying to research stocks on their lunch break or to calculate potential returns after work. They do this all day, every day, and the professional investor will always be better at it than you can be.

YOUR COMPETITIVE EDGE

Investing is not a hobby to be dabbled in hoping for good results. It's a competitive, zero-sum game.

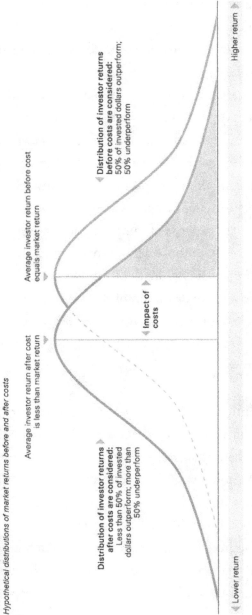

The impact of costs on overall investor returns
Hypothetical distributions of market returns before and after costs

Average investor return after cost is less than market return

Distribution of investor returns after costs are considered:
Less than 50% of invested dollars outperform; more than 50% underperform

Average investor return before cost equals market return

Distribution of investor returns before costs are considered:
50% of invested dollars outperform; 50% underperform

Impact of costs

◀ Lower return

Higher return ▶

Note: These distributions are theoretical and do not reflect any set of actual returns. Source: Vanguard.

The chart above illustrates that the average investor's return has to equal the market's return, since the market consists of the combined outcomes of all investors, minus investment costs. Therefore, your outperformance has to come at someone else's expense by a wide enough margin to cover your costs. You need to be a significantly above-average investor to poach someone else's fair share of returns.

Howard Marks, co-chairman of Oaktree Capital and someone with an incredible investment track record, has much to say about this in his book *The Most Important Thing Illuminated: Uncommon Sense for the Thoughtful Investor*. It's a must-read for anyone considering managing their own assets. Marks warns that, in the competitive investment landscape, where your above-average return has to come at the expense of someone's below-average return, success will come only to those who devote serious time and have the intellectual firepower and depth of thinking to beat the herd. This isn't a shallow warning. Millions of the brightest minds will pursue the same goals with access to the same information and tools to beat you. What's your edge? When you make an investment decision, what do you think you know that the person trading against you doesn't?

Similar difficulties apply if you forgo investing in individual stocks and bonds and instead choose ETFs or mutual funds. There are more of these than there are publicly traded stocks; how are you going to choose well? Past performance, star ratings, and recommended best funds lists have all proven woefully inadequate at identifying good investments. Professional investment teams devote significant resources and time searching for diamonds in the rough. What will be your edge as you try to uncover whether one fund or strategy can deliver consistently impressive returns?

In 2007, Warren Buffett made a bet with Protégé Partners, a money manager that runs fund of funds hedge fund strategies. A hedge fund is a less-regulated investment vehicle available only to accredited investors (must meet certain criteria established by the Securities and Exchange Commission to denote financial sophistication) who can employ a wide range of strategies and invest in a broad set of assets to achieve their stated objective. If that sounds somewhat vague, it is, since it's become more of an investment type than a strategy. A fund of funds is a hedge fund made up of other underlying hedge funds chosen by a manager.

Buffett's bet was simple. Protégé Partners would win if the ten-year performance of five funds of funds outperformed the S&P 500 Index fund that Buffett believed would do better. The wager ended in 2017. The index fund returned 7.1 percent per year. The hedge funds earned a measly 2.2 percent by comparison.[18]

I share this story for a couple of reasons. First, the poor performance of the hedge funds themselves should give potential do-it-yourself investors pause. While the funds' names weren't disclosed, they were sophisticated stock investors who tried to beat the market and failed. It's true that part of Buffett's theory was his belief that hedge funds' large fees would prove a headwind and that someone running their own portfolio wouldn't face these fees. But the extent of the underperformance means it wasn't just fees that hurt. The investment experts didn't perform well. Second, the inability of professionals—in this instance, people whose business model it is to choose good hedge funds for their clients—to identify hedge funds that would perform well over a ten-year period should cause you to

---

18   Emily Price, "Warren Buffett Just Won a $1 million Bet," *Fortune*, December 30, 2017, https://fortune.com/2017/12/30/warren-buffett-million-dollar-bet.

question your ability to pick good mutual funds or ETFs yourself. Protégé Partners had a huge incentive to win this bet. The free publicity alone from such a high-stakes wager with the world's foremost investor would likely be a greater benefit than any marketing program they could create. And losing such a public contest would hurt their business. But lose they did.

The larger point is that this story isn't some cherry-picked anomaly; it's the norm. Professional investors struggle mightily to outperform the markets they're trying to beat. If you're an investment junkie, it's a well-known and oft-told story. Study after study has shown that mutual fund managers—the broadest class of professional investors out there—haven't done well relative to the benchmarks they're measured against. Ending 2017, 92.33 percent of large cap managers, 94.81 percent of mid cap managers, and 95.73 percent of small cap managers underperformed their benchmark over the previous fifteen years.[19] As I said, it's not a new story. But what you do with it could be.

Many investors hear this and decide that they're going to forgo paying fees for a portfolio that will likely underperform the markets. Better to just do it themselves, since the pros can't get it done either. That's the wrong takeaway. When a large group of very smart, experienced, and highly paid professionals with major incentives to outperform their peers can't do it, what makes you think *Oh boy, I can't wait to compete with these folks*? What edge do you think you have that they don't? Rather than disrespect their abilities to the point where you think you can beat them without their training and experience while doing it part-time, I urge you instead to respect the difficulty of beating the markets and avoid wading in on your own.

---

19   Mark Perry, "More evidence that it's very hard to 'beat the market' over time, 95% of finance professionals can't do it," AEI.org, March 4, 2018, https://www.aei.org/carpe-diem/more-evidence-that-its-very-hard-to-beat-the-market-over-time-95-of-financial-professionals-cant-do-it.

This leads to a second takeaway from the dismal performance stats above. Because professional investors struggle to outperform their benchmarks, many investors have decided to invest in index funds that mirror the benchmarks' performance minus small fees and costs. Again, you investment junkies already know about the shift from active managers who are trying to beat a benchmark to passive investment strategies like index funds and index-tracking ETFs. It's been a mammoth shift over the years and, in many ways, is a rational response to high-fee managers underperforming cheap index funds. However, it's not the panacea it has been touted as, which leads to our third reason why it makes sense to work with an advisor instead of managing your own money.

DISTANCING YOUR INVESTMENTS FROM EMOTION

Maybe I'm preaching to the choir. Let's say you get it and have decided to index. You'll ditch the hassle of trying to beat the market, either through picking your own individual securities or by picking funds or managers to outperform. You understand that if the average investor earns the market return minus fees, taking the market return through low-cost index funds puts you ahead.

This is also what Warren Buffett would have you do based on his instructions to his wife's trustee: "Put 10% of the cash in short-term government bonds and 90% in a very low-cost S&P 500 index fund. (I suggest Vanguard's.) I believe the trust's long-term results from this policy will be superior to those attained by most investors."[20]

However, if earning your fair share of the market's return were that easy, wouldn't everyone just index and do great? Of course, but

---

20 Berkshire Hathaway Corporation, *Annual Report 2013*, retrieved from https://www. berkshirehathaway.com/letters/letters.html.

they don't. This is overly simplistic advice solving the wrong investor problem. The biggest obstacle individual investors face isn't that their investments perform poorly or cost more; it's that they make poor investment-timing decisions. They succumb to fear and greed. Overcoming that is more important than what investment strategy you choose, and index funds don't help the timing issue.

In late 2008, I worked at a mid-size money manager in Rochester, New York, named Manning & Napier Advisors. I was the managing director of its Family Wealth Management group, which was responsible for providing ongoing financial planning to about four hundred of the firm's largest individual clients. Our main challenge then was keeping clients focused on their long-term goals during a historic market decline. We didn't want them panic-selling out of the market close to the bottom, and we were doing well at it.

However, thousands of other clients weren't receiving our services, and I didn't want them selling at the wrong time either. I asked the firm's president how I could help, and he suggested presenting arguments to stay the course at our upcoming seminar series about the market crisis.

Here's the gist of what I said.

People make poor investment decisions. They succumb to fear and greed and ignore their long-term objectives. In 2008, we were worried about fear, but both emotions can be devastating.

In 1999, we were at the tail end of an amazing bull market. The market returned 37.2 percent in 1995, 22.68 percent in 1996, 33.10 percent in 1997, 28.34 percent in 1998, and 20.89 percent in 1999. That makes five straight years of the market smashing its long-term historical return of 10 percent. How did investors react? They invested a then record $174,456,000,000 into stock mutual funds. Instead of getting nervous about a historically expensive market, they piled in. Their reward? In 2000, the market declined by 9.03 percent. In 2001, the decline was 11.85 percent. And in 2002, the decline reached 21.97 percent. And how did investors react to that bear market? Did they view it as a buying opportunity, since the stocks they loved at record highs were now significantly cheaper? In 2002, they added only $19,594,000,000 to stock mutual funds—a mere 10 percent of what they were investing at record highs. In 2003, the market returned 28.67 percent.

Fast-forward to 2008. The market declined 36.55 percent. Investors withdrew a then record $147,321,000,000 from stock mutual funds. The market's return in 2009 was 25.94 percent, and the masses of investors who had sold out of the market the previous year missed those gains.

All the indexing in the world won't fix poor timing decisions. History shows that you won't stay put during market extremes. You'll either get greedy at the wrong time, or you'll get fearful when you're not supposed to. Buy low and sell high becomes buy high and sell low and allows other investors to take your fair share of market returns. With every seller having a buyer, panicking during market declines transfers some of your future returns to the unemotional buyer.

The independent investment research firm Morningstar provides an interesting look at performance. It tracks total returns and investor returns for mutual funds. Here's Morningstar's explanation:

> Investors often suffer from poor timing and poor planning. Investors know they should hold diversified portfolios, but many chase past performance and end up buying funds too late or selling too soon.
>
> A fund's published total return reflects a buy and hold strategy. . . . But not all investors buy and hold. Investors move their money in and out of funds as they search for the best return.

In contrast to total return, investor return accounts for all cash flows into and out of the fund to measure how the average investor performed over time. In a classic example, a fund receives a great inflow of assets right after a period of good performance and right before a period of poor performance. . . . In this example, investor return is lower than total return because more investors participated in the losses.

To use one example highlighted below, how have investors in Vanguard's flagship S&P 500 Index fund performed relative to how the fund itself has performed? Poorly. Over the past fifteen years, they have underperformed by 1.92 percent. An initial investment of $100,000 in the fund should have ended up being $254,660, but investors only received $193,806—31.4 percent less. The ten-year number also lags. You will note that the one-, three-, and five-year investor returns are stronger than the total return. That seemingly undercuts the argument, but these are also the time periods that do not include a bear market. The ten-year number includes the 2007–2009 bear market, and the fifteen-year number includes that one plus some of the 2000–2002 bear market.

TRAILING INVESTOR RETURNS VFINX

Monthly					
Trailing Returns (08/31/2016)	1-Year	3-Year	5-Year	10-Year	15-year
Investor Return %	12.14	12.66	15.23	4.81	4.51
Total Return %	12.39	12.14	14.51	7.39	6.43
% Rank in Category (INV Rtn)	14	8	9	57	49

Source: Morningstar

Numerous studies have shown similar things. The table below summarizes the findings of one, with specific categories broken out.[21]

COMPARISON OF DOLLAR- AND TIME-WEIGHTED RETURNS FOR MUTUAL FUND PORTFOLIOS BASED ON FUND TYPE (JANUARY 1991–JUNE 2013)

Fund Classification	Dollar Weighted Return	Buy & Hold Return	Difference (DW Ret – TW Ret)	p-Value On Difference
S&P 500 Total Return				
Index		9.53%		
All Funds	6.87%	8.81%	−1.94%	0.000
Growth Funds	5.22%	8.38%	−3.16%	0.000
Value Funds	8.05%	9.36%	1.31%	0.003
Small-Cap Funds	8.23%	9.78%	−1.55%	0.000
Large-Cap Funds	6.76%	8.66%	−1.90%	0.000
Index Funds	6.95%	9.66%	−2.72%	0.003
Active Funds	6.85%	9.73%	−1.88%	0.000

This table reports buy-and-hold vs. dollar-weighted return portfolios of different categories of mutual funds weighted by total net assets. The buy-and-hold return is the geometric average return over the sample period. The dollar-weighted return is the IRR of the category (inclusive of all mutual funds in the category weighted by their total assets), calculated as in Dichev (2007). The difference between the dollar-weighted and buy-and-hold return is reported. Also reported is a derived p-value estimated from bootstrap tests under the null hypothesis that the difference between the realized dollar-weighted and time-weighted return is not statistically different from the difference between a random dollar-weighted return and the realized time-weighted return.

Source: Research Affiliates using data from the CRSP Mutual Funds Database and Morningstar Direct

---

21   *Timing Poorly: A Guide to Generating Poor Returns While Investing in Successful Strategies.*

The investor return gap is persistent. Indexing doesn't fix this gap for you, and going it alone exposes you to it. It's not necessary to be a skilled investor in order to increase your net worth and accomplish your financial goals. Strong capital allocation decision-making skills are much more important, and investing in a traditional portfolio is just one tool you can use.

It's also a tool easily accessed through professional help from others. I urge you to consider this path for the reasons discussed above. Namely, you likely do not have an investment edge that makes it reasonable for you to compete with the multitude of professional investors you will be buying and selling from, and without help, you are likely to succumb to the dual curses of fear and greed. An advisor puts distance between your emotions and your investment decisions.

FINDING THE RIGHT ADVISOR

Congratulations. You've made a decision on which direction to go with your portfolio management and have decided to hire an advisor. Now comes finding that advisor. Like all professions, there are advisors who do a great job that you'll be lucky to work with, there are awful advisors who could hurt your finances, and there's every level in between. It can get bewildering, but fortunately, there are five things you can do outside of getting a strong referral from someone who knows you to find the advisor who's the right fit.

To find the right advisor:

- Target the right scope of services.
- Use the right type of advisor and research them.
- Make sure they have the right credentials.

- Start things off the right way.

- Understand their approach.

THE RIGHT SCOPE OF SERVICES

First, find an advisor who provides comprehensive financial planning services in addition to portfolio management. The best advisors offer both for a fee of 1 percent or less of the assets they manage. The ones you shouldn't be working with are caught up in the past and either charge more or charge the same but offer minimal financial planning advice. Believe me, we're still seeing too much of both.

This begs the question: If you've never worked with an advisor before, how do you know if the financial planning services of the advisor you're considering are comprehensive? There's no strict definition, but a comprehensive planner will want to learn about your background and current situation, understand your goals and objectives, figure out what you're trying to do long-term with the money you're investing, create some sort of cash-flow model or retirement plan to guide future decisions, advise you on whether you have sufficient insurance coverage, make sure you're saving in the right places, can provide tax planning suggestions, and will discuss your estate plan and charitable goals. Most important, they do all of this proactively and meet or speak with you multiple times a year to keep the plan on track.

THE RIGHT TYPE OF ADVISOR

Second, find a fee-based fiduciary to be your advisor instead of a broker. I know: jargon alert. But understanding these terms is key. A fiduciary is required to provide advice in your best interests and disclose any possible conflicts of interest. Their compensation is typically based on a fee tied to the assets they manage (the 1 percent or less from above) or some kind of hourly or fixed planning fee. They are not licensed to sell anything like commission-based mutual funds or insurance and, therefore, do not make any money from selling products to you. They are also usually independent, which means their firm does not manage proprietary investment products in-house, so they are free to recommend the best investment for your situation.

A broker is held to a lower standard, known as the suitability standard. To meet that standard, a broker's recommendation need only be suitable for the client. No conflict of interest disclosures need to be made. It doesn't require finding the best or cheapest investment, just something appropriate for your situation. They also don't have to tell you that they are recommending it because it pays them more. For example, if you are a growth-oriented investor, they need to merely recommend a mutual fund (or group of mutual funds) that is appropriate for a growth-oriented investor. If it is more expensive than another fund they could be investing you in, they do not need to explain that or alter their recommendation. If they are recommending it because it is their company's mutual fund, that is okay. If they are getting paid more to recommend this fund over others, that's not something you'll see in their presentation to you.

Related to this is the necessity to research the advisor you're considering. Their own website is a fine place to start, but beyond the general package of information put together by the advisor, check out their public filings and determine whether they have any customer complaints or violations. The investment advisor public disclosure site maintained by the Securities and Exchange Commission (SEC) is the place to go—adviserinfo.sec.gov—to be able to read the firm's Form ADV and check their compliance history. Form ADV is required to be submitted and updated to the SEC annually for any advisory firm that manages more than $25 million. It contains information about the firm's key personnel, assets under management, services provided, fees charged, investment strategy, and any past disciplinary action that may have been taken against the advisor.

THE RIGHT CREDENTIALS

Since we've already established that you want an advisor who does planning and investing, it's important to make sure they have the right credentials to do both. The financial planning services should be provided by a CERTIFIED FINANCIAL PLANNER® and the portfolios should be managed by Chartered Financial Analyst® charterholders. There are plenty of qualified planners without the CFP® and portfolio managers without a CFA®, and there are plenty of morons with those credentials. However, these are credentials of record for their respective industries, and they demonstrate professional commitment, the proper educational background, mastery of requisite core knowledge, and the ability to pass difficult qualifying exams, and they have continuing educational requirements and strict ethical standards.

To earn the CFP® certification, you have to complete the CFP® Board of Standards' education requirements in the financial planning areas listed below, develop a financial plan, and pass a difficult comprehensive exam that, in 2017, had a 64 percent pass rate.

- Professional conduct and regulation
- General principles of financial planning
- Education planning

- Risk management and insurance planning
- Investment planning
- Tax planning
- Retirement savings and income planning
- Estate planning

The CFA® program is a rigorous graduate-level program that takes at least four years to complete and more than three hundred hours of studying per level. There are three levels, and the historic pass rate for each is between 40 percent and 60 percent. Those levels cover economics, corporate finance, investments, quantitative modeling, financial reporting and analysis, various investment asset classes, ethics, portfolio management, and wealth planning.

START THINGS OFF CORRECTLY

The right advisor should want to start the investment process with you by creating a financial plan to guide your investment strategy and future decisions. The CFA Institute recommends that investment advisors create an investment policy statement (IPS) that covers investment objectives, risk management, and any portfolio constraints the advisor should adhere to based on client preferences. The goals are agreed on, the time horizon is understood, and the monitoring criteria and investment expectations are discussed.

An IPS is a great idea but is more common with institutional clients like large pension plans and charitable foundations. A detailed financial plan accomplishes many of the same things. It will model future portfolio contributions, the time horizon until withdrawals, withdrawal amounts, how earnings and withdrawals will be taxed, and so much more.

The right advisor's approach should be to use a financial plan they create with you to set your portfolio's asset allocation—the amount of money you have invested in stocks, bonds, cash, or other asset classes—which is the key driver of future returns. There's a famous study from 1995 that's touted ad nauseam by financial professionals as claiming that asset allocation accounts for 93.6 percent of a portfolio's return. The study doesn't exactly phrase it that way, but in "Determinants of Portfolio Performance," Gary P. Brinson, L. Randolph Hood, and Gilbert L. Beebower concluded that investment policy (the long-term asset allocation plan and what would be considered normal weights assigned to each asset class) proved much more important to returns than market timing and investment selection.

If the advisor you are considering has a different approach to getting started that does not focus on understanding your goals and building out a plan, then I would recommend interviewing others. Find one who doesn't invest money in a vacuum but only after understanding what the money needs to be used for and when.

UNDERSTAND THEIR APPROACH

Another way to give yourself the best chance for success when working with an advisor is to make sure they have an investment philosophy you understand and can remain committed to for the long term (especially during market distress). Understanding the investment philosophy involves knowing who the investment team is, how they select investments and make asset allocation decisions, their view on portfolio expectations, and how the portfolio will react in different markets. Many different approaches can work. What doesn't work is the absence of a plan or changing course at the first bit of uncertainty. The discipline to remain committed to your plan means as much as the plan itself and can only be attained if you enter a long-term relationship with a clear understanding of what your advisor's core investment beliefs are.

The following discussion of the things I like most about my firm's investment approach can help you understand the level of knowledge you should have about your own advisor's philosophy.

My firm's approach can be explained well in the context of all of the recent chatter pushing people to invest in cheap index funds since active managers cannot outperform. It's hard to argue with the data.

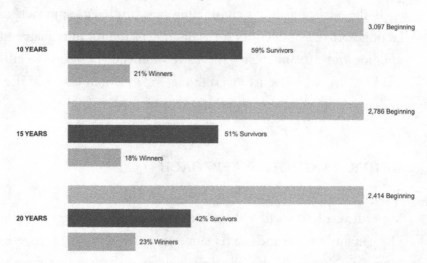

Few Equity Funds Have Survived and Outperformed

US-based equity fund performance periods ending December 31, 2018

10 YEARS
3,097 Beginning
59% Survivors
21% Winners

15 YEARS
2,786 Beginning
51% Survivors
18% Winners

20 YEARS
2,414 Beginning
42% Survivors
23% Winners

Source: Dimensional Fund Advisors LP. The sample includes funds at the beginning of the 10-, 15-, and 20-year periods ending December 31, 2018. Survivors are funds that had returns for every month in the sample period. Winners are funds that survived and outperformed their benchmark over the period. US domiciled open-end mutual fund data is from Morningstar. Past performance is no guarantee of future results.

For the five-, ten-, and fifteen-year time periods shown above, a mutual fund had better odds of going out of business than outperforming its index, and the overwhelming majority underperformed. Myriad theories exist about why, but theories only matter in ivory towers and conference rooms. They contain great phrases like *paradox of skill*, *efficient markets*, *active share*, and *benchmark hugging*, but you're trying to figure out how to invest. We can save the theories for later.

Many investors have focused on one primary reason for underperformance: Active managers cost more, and those fees are a performance drag that cannot be overcome. Once again, the numbers don't lie. More expensive managers do not perform as well.

High Costs Can Reduce Performance

US-based equity fund winners and losers based on expense ratios (%)

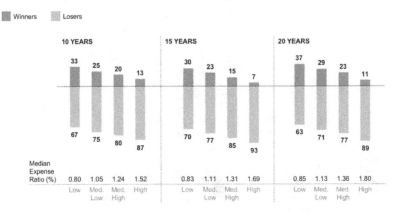

Source: Dimensional Fund Advisors LP. The sample includes funds at the beginning of the 10-, 15-, and 20-year periods ending December 31, 2018. Survivors are funds that had returns for every month in the sample period. Winners are funds that survived and outperformed their benchmark over the period. US domiciled open-end mutual fund data is from Morningstar. Past performance is no guarantee of future results.

The lower the fee, the better chance you have to outperform the market and vice versa. Some investors have pushed this to its logical extent and plowed money into index funds. If outperformance is difficult and paying less means earning more, it's a rational response.

However, for some reason, it leaves me lacking, and not because I have some career-conflicting aversion to it. Our firm could use index funds for our clients if we believed in them. Don't get me wrong; there are things I like about index funds. Lower-fee and lower-turn-over approaches make sense. Our firm uses strategies that meet these criteria as well. Lower-turnover funds that keep costs down by placing fewer trades and that are more tax-efficient help investors keep more of what they earn.

High Trading Costs Can Also Impact Returns

US-based equity fund winners and losers based on turnover (%)

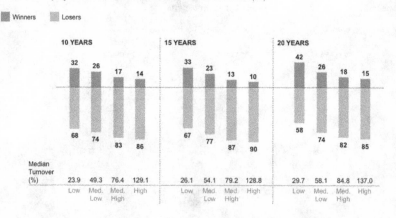

Source: Dimensional Fund Advisors LP. The sample includes funds at the beginning of the 10-, 15-, and 20-year periods ending December 31, 2018. Survivors are funds that had returns for every month in the sample period. Winners are funds that survived and outperformed their benchmark over the period. US domiciled open-end mutual fund data is from Morningstar. Past performance is no guarantee of future results.

However, boiling investments down to one variable—fees— doesn't make sense to me. There are things about indexing I don't like. The biggest one is that the index doesn't care about price. I'm price-conscious in everything I do. People call me cheap, but I prefer to say I appreciate value. I've been conditioned to believe (and handle my financial life accordingly) that what you pay for something matters. I just can't love an investment approach that forces me to own more of what's expensive and less of what's cheap.

How excited would you be to invest with a manager that had 29.2 percent of its portfolio in technology stocks in 1999, right before the bubble in technology stocks burst? Since technology stocks had performed so well for so long, they grew to be a disproportionate part of the S&P 500 Index, and index fund investors had to own those massively overpriced stocks in that large percentage. The opposite happened with energy stocks. Oil prices had bottomed out to $16.42, so those stocks were doing so poorly that only 6.3 percent of the index was invested in the cheap energy stocks. Index investors had too little invested in energy and missed the rebound that came in those stocks as oil prices climbed to a peak of $144.78 in 2008. In 2007, the financial sector had grown so much due to the real estate bubble that subsequently popped in spectacular fashion that index investors were forced to invest 22.3 percent of their portfolio in those overpriced stocks.

Historical sector weightings of the S&P 500: 1990–2019

Sector	1990	1993	1996	1998	1999	2000	2001	2002	2004	2006	2007	2008	3/09	2009	2010	2011
Tech	6.3	5.9	12.4	17.7	29.2	21.2	17.6	14.3	16.1	15.1	16.7	15.3	17.6	19.9	18.7	19.0
Financials	7.5	11.2	15.0	15.4	13.0	17.3	17.8	20.5	20.6	22.3	17.6	13.3	8.9	14.4	16.1	13.4
Energy	13.4	10.0	9.2	6.3	5.6	6.6	6.3	6.0	7.2	9.8	12.9	13.3	14.3	11.5	12.0	12.3
H. Care	10.4	8.2	10.4	12.3	9.3	14.4	14.4	14.9	12.7	12.0	12.0	14.8	16.1	12.6	10.9	11.9
Cons Stap	14.0	12.5	12.7	11.1	7.2	8.1	8.2	9.5	10.5	9.3	10.2	12.9	13.8	11.4	10.6	11.5
Industrials	13.6	13.9	12.7	10.1	9.9	10.6	11.3	11.5	11.8	10.8	11.5	11.1	9.5	10.3	11.0	10.7
Cons Disc	12.8	16.4	11.7	12.5	12.7	10.3	13.1	13.4	11.9	10.6	8.5	8.4	8.3	9.6	10.6	10.7
Materials	7.2	7.1	5.8	3.1	3.0	2.3	2.6	2.8	3.1	3.0	3.3	2.9	3.2	3.6	3.7	3.5
Utilities	6.2	5.6	3.7	3.0	2.2	3.8	3.1	2.9	2.9	3.6	3.6	4.2	4.4	3.7	3.3	3.9
Telecom	8.7	9.1	6.5	8.4	7.9	5.5	5.5	4.2	3.3	3.5	3.6	3.8	4.0	3.2	3.1	3.2

Source: http://quant.stackexchange.com/questions/4115/sp500-sector-weights-how-do-they-change

Indexing is fine until it isn't. When the market tumbles, it tends to tumble from the top down, meaning the most expensive sectors or stocks feel more than their fair share of the market decline. The technology sector had gone from 29.2 percent of the S&P 500 in 1999 to 14.3 percent in 2002. Financials had moved from 22.3 percent in 2006 to 8.9 percent at the market bottom in March 2009.

I'd prefer to factor price into my investment decisions to avoid concentrating my portfolio in expensive sectors and buy cheaper ones. I'd also like to do it in a way that still retains some of the advantages of indexing (low fees, lower turnover, and tax efficiency), so I can keep more of what I earn from the markets.

That's what our firm is looking to do in our portfolios: a low-cost investment experience that factors in price, still has lower fees and portfolio turnover, and does a few other things that make sense for our clients, which gives them a reasonable opportunity to extract maximum performance from the markets. Rather than blindly buying an index (or a set of indexes) and delinking our client portfolios from any definition of value, our firm prefers to have our clients' stock allocations be exposed to certain things that have rewarded investors over time.

The first is value. Historically, value stocks have outperformed growth stocks by an average of 4.7 percent between 1928 and 2014. This outperformance does not come every year but has been available to the long-term investor.

Second, investors have been rewarded for investing in smaller companies. Smaller companies can more easily grow their capital at higher rates than larger companies can. Warren Buffett explains this in one of his shareholder letters: "An iron law of business is that growth eventually dampens exceptional economics. Just look at the records of high-return companies once they have amassed even

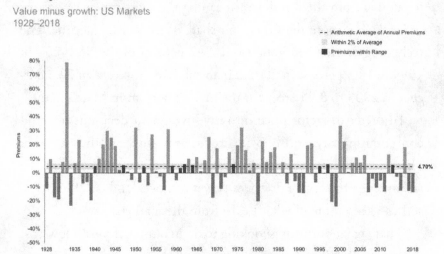

Yearly Observations of Premiums
Value minus growth: US Markets
1928–2018

Source: Dimensional Fund Advisors LP. The value premium is the Fama/French HML factor: (Fama/French US Small Value and US Large Value Research Indexes) minus (Fama/French US Small Growth and US Large Growth Research Indexes). Fama/French indexes provided by Ken French. Index descriptions available upon request. Indexes are not available for direct investment. Their performance does not reflect the expenses associated with the management of an actual portfolio. Past performance is no guarantee of future results. Eugene Fama and Ken French are members of the board of directors for and provide consulting services to Dimensional Fund Advisors LP.

$1 billion of equity capital. None that I know of has managed subsequently, over a 10-year period, to keep on earning 20% or more on equity while reinvesting all or substantially all of its earnings."[22]

Consider your own situation. Do you think it'll be easier for you to grow your net worth by 20 percent when you have a net worth of $100,000 or when it is $1 million?

---

22 Berkshire Hathaway Corporation, *Annual Report 1985*, retrieved from https://www.berkshirehathaway.com/letters/letters.html.

Small cap minus large cap:
US markets 1928–2018

Yearly Observations of Premiums

Small cap minus large cap: US Markets
1928–2018

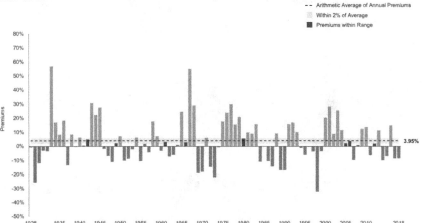

Source: Dimensional Fund Advisors LP. The size premium is the Fama/French SMB factor: (Fama/French US Small Value, US Small Neutral, and US Small Growth Research Indexes) minus (Fama/French US Large Value, US Large Neutral, and US Large Growth Research Indexes). Fama/French indexes provided by Ken French. Index descriptions available upon request. Indexes are not available for direct investment. Their performance does not reflect the expenses associated with the management of an actual portfolio. Past performance is no guarantee of future results. Eugene Fama and Ken French are members of the board of directors for and provide consulting services to Dimensional Fund Advisors LP.

Our firm currently has a higher allocation to small cap stocks in its clients' portfolios than the market indexes to try and take advantage of that 3.95 percent outperformance.

Third, profitable companies have historically outperformed less-profitable ones.

High profitability minus low profitability: US markets 1964–2018

Yearly Observations of Premiums

High profitability minus low profitability: US Markets
1964–2018

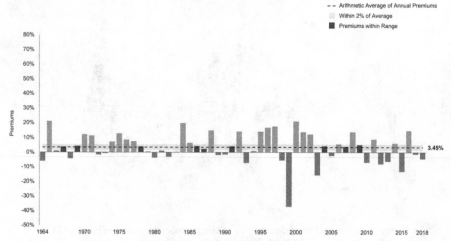

- - Arithmetic Average of Annual Premiums
  Within 2% of Average
  Premiums within Range

3.45%

Source: Dimensional Fund Advisors LP. The profitability premium is the Fama/French RMW factor: (Fama/French US Small Robust and US Large Robust Profitability Research Indexes) minus (Fama/French US Small Weak and US Large Weak Profitability Research Indexes). Profitability is measured as operating income before depreciation and amortization minus interest expense, scaled by book. Fama/French indexes provided by Ken French. Index descriptions available upon request. Indexes are not available for direct investment. Their performance does not reflect the expenses associated with the management of an actual portfolio. Past performance is no guarantee of future results. Eugene Fama and Ken French are members of the board of directors for and provide consulting services to Dimensional Fund Advisors LP.

Focusing on cheaper stocks, smaller companies, and profitable companies is somewhat of a no-brainer, perhaps. However, indexing doesn't do that for you. Indexes are typically market cap weighted, which means that the bigger the company, the more you own. In addition, the stronger the performance of the stock, the more you own.

Instead of building stock portfolios around one variable, our firm takes a more balanced approach. We use low-cost funds that have low turnover but expect our managers not to ignore commonsense pricing and structural advantages that could help our clients in the globally diversified portfolios we build for them.

How much we invest in stocks is based on our clients' financial plans and the current market environment. Historically, stocks have outperformed other asset classes, and we want to expose clients to stocks to the extent we can, given their long-term goals and current valuations. However, this stronger return potential comes with significantly higher short-term volatility and risk of short-term loss, so clients usually need to own other asset classes. The exact allocation to those asset classes depends on clients' time horizons, withdrawal needs, and the investment environment. For stability and income, we usually add bonds, whose quality and duration depends on our views of the bond market at the time. Similar to our stock investing, we focus on price and risk and reward in the current investment climate.

Selecting risk profile in the fixed-income market

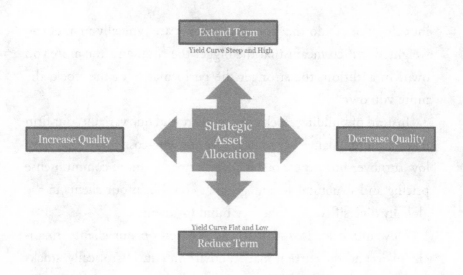

Source: Heritage Financial Investment Committee

Our firm prefers to invest in lower-quality bonds when credit spreads widen and investors are paid to own them. We can then increase quality when we are not being paid to take the risk. Similarly, we prefer to own longer-term bonds when the yield curve is steep and we expect to be compensated for the duration risk. We prefer to own shorter-term bonds in the opposite scenario.

For diversification and a different source of positive return, our firm will complement these two asset classes with alternative investments that meet the following criteria: a positive expected long-term return relative to the stocks and bonds used to fund them and investments that shouldn't move in tandem with the stock and bond markets or each other so they are providing portfolio diversification and risk management.

In summary, I believe focusing on fees is appropriate, but limiting your investment philosophy to just one variable doesn't make sense when it forces you to ignore price discovery and the fundamentals that could lead to a higher return. You need to have a framework for investing in bonds, since they can provide stability and protection during market declines. Select alternative investments may add value in the right situations. The exact mix of how much you have in all three (your asset allocation) should be guided by your financial plan and personal situation.

CHECK THE BAROMETER

A traditional investment portfolio can be the cornerstone of your capital allocation strategy. At the very least, it can serve as a good barometer for the level of returns available to you as you consider alternatives. I've called traditional market returns accessible and hassle-free, but that does not mean they are easy to get. Most of us should consider working with an advisor to manage our portfolios, because it's a time-consuming task that can be easily outsourced, markets are competitive, and you need protection from the powerful emotions of fear and greed.

Make sure your advisor offers financial planning, as well as investment management. Look for fiduciaries and do the appropriate due diligence. Work with advisory firms where the people doing your planning and investing have the right credentials. Find someone who wants to start things off by building a financial plan to guide the investment process, and understand their investment approach so you can remain committed to it long-term. Finding the right advisor may not be easy, but if you seek out these criteria, you'll be more likely to succeed.

CHAPTER 7

DIY Investing

"Keep it simple, stupid."

—Design principle of the US Navy

I'd like to think you're convinced that the challenges of doing it yourself—namely, of having enough skill to compete and of avoiding the deleterious siren song of market timing—make hiring an advisor the obvious way to go. Nevertheless, some of you won't agree, because you find investing interesting, are ultra fee-conscious, or are just skeptical of the financial services industry. This chapter contains more information to consider before choosing a path, although it could be used as a do-it-yourself guide. To be clear, *I do not recommend this path.* You are better off with an advisor. However, I'm confident we can help you avoid the worst results by adopting the KISS principle quoted above.

KISS—for *keep it simple, stupid*—is a design principle focused on simplicity. Systems work better by avoiding unnecessary complexity. The complexity, in this case, comes from overconfidently chasing a portfolio approach that'll burn you. A great way to get burned is acting like you have expertise you don't. Let this quote mistakenly attributed to Mark Twain be your guide: "It ain't what you don't know that gets you in trouble. It's what you know for sure that just ain't so."

I'm not trying to be condescending or dismissive by laying it out this way; I'm being realistic. We've already discussed how much skill and expertise it takes to compete in the investment marketplace, not including the major concerns I have over your ability to stick with a portfolio once you've built it. The more complex approaches, like picking your own stocks or building portfolios with multiple asset classes, require professional talent, so why compete on their playing field when there is a simpler way?

PICKING STOCKS

To build a stock portfolio, you must do the analysis described in the following paragraphs enough times to be diversified, in case one or two picks go bad. Determining that number could lead us down a big rabbit hole, so for now, let's say twenty, meaning each stock will be 5 percent of your stock portfolio.

First, develop and run an initial screen on the thousands of stocks to identify candidates for further analysis. You'll need to know what type of stocks you're targeting and why: cheap, strong growth, smaller stocks, dividend payers, and so on. All approaches have proponents, and all require different initial screens.

Next, analyze the names and review each balance sheet. What are the company's assets and liabilities? Is it financially healthy, or is there too much debt? Are the assets liquid or illiquid, and is the debt short-term or long-term? Can the company pay its short-term liabilities with its liquid current assets?

Review each company's income statement and cash-flow statement to assess profitability, cash-flow generation, returns on assets, and whether it is cheap or expensive relative to its prospects. That last piece involves an ability to understand the business and its competitors and to assess where it's going.

The goal of all of this is to determine whether the stock is a buy, to understand what you're paying and why, and to develop monitoring points to track as future news, earnings reports, and public filings come out to ensure your investment thesis is tracking the right way.

This brings us to selling. You need a sell discipline. Assuming you're able to do the work above, when will you sell your stocks? Will it be when your thesis doesn't play out, the stock is too expensive, it becomes too big a percentage of your portfolio, you find a better idea, or it drops a certain percentage?

As you can see, there's a lot of work and expertise required here. And the cost of failure is high: permanently lost capital that you've spent years acquiring. Why risk it?

ASSET ALLOCATION

So we're not stock picking, unless of course you're one of the few who have the skillset. That leaves asset allocation as a way to invest. Asset allocation is the process of deciding which asset classes to invest in and in what percentages. Investopedia defines an asset class as a group of securities that exhibit similar characteristics, behave similarly in the marketplace, and are subject to the same laws and resolutions. Stocks, bonds, and cash are the most widely known and understood. Others include real estate, commodities, and precious metals.

The purpose of asset allocation is to invest in asset classes with different risk and return characteristics that do not historically move in lockstep. *All About Asset Allocation*, by Richard A. Ferri, explains it this way: "Asset allocation is a type of diversification that spreads the risk widely over different markets."[23] You'll want to estimate the expected risks and returns of different parts of the financial markets and build a portfolio with those parts in a way that makes your investment vulnerable to the least risk but subject to the highest return. Done correctly, it requires serious but different investment skills than stock picking:

- The ability to make return estimates for various asset classes

- An understanding of correlation combined with the know-how to assess different asset class correlations

- Determining in which percentages to own multiple asset classes to build a diversified portfolio that can provide strong risk-adjusted returns tailored to meet your goals

If you can do these things, great. Go for it and skip ahead. If you can't, why are we setting you up for failure? Let's simplify this in two ways. First, we'll focus only on the core asset classes of cash, bonds, and stocks. Second, we'll let time horizon, which is more easily understood, be our guide.

---

23   Richard A. Ferri, *All About Asset Allocation* (New York: McGraw-Hill, 2010), 41.

BUCKETING

Our KISS framework is going to be what is sometimes called the bucket approach. Understanding bucketing is easier if you review our work so far. We've built up to making long-term investments by making sure that you don't have bad debts to pay off before you start saving and investing, that your spending is under control so you won't have to tap into your savings to feed consumption, and that you've set enough aside in a rainy day fund to cover unanticipated short-term spending needs or emergencies. Only after accomplishing those steps did we pivot to the long term.

Bucketing is investing pools of money based on when you'll need them. You avoid withdrawing money from a bucket that has temporarily declined in value, which would lock in a permanent loss. The three most common buckets are these:

- Short-term needs
- Long-term needs
- Intermediate needs

SHORT-TERM BUCKET

Your short-term bucket is money you'll need in the next three years, and it should be in cash. Cash is the only fully liquid guaranteed investment. CDs are guaranteed but not liquid. Bonds are liquid but not guaranteed. Find a high-yield savings account (a money market fund with a decent yield), set it aside, and call it a day.

LONG-TERM BUCKET

Your long-term bucket should be for money you won't need for more than 15 years. This is longer than you might think and, indeed, longer than most proponents of the bucketing approach advocate. There are two reasons to plan that far out:

- The risk of loss
- To be aggressive

Risk of loss

According to price history on the S&P 500, a broad stock market index that tracks the performance of large US company stocks, to be certain that you won't experience a market loss during your holding period, you should have a 100 percent stock portfolio if your holding period is sixteen years. I know breaking even over that long a stretch isn't your goal. Don't worry: The average annual return for a sixteen-year portfolio is more than 9 percent, the best is close to 20 percent, and the worst is still positive.

Be aggressive

This is long-term money that needs to grow, so invest it aggressively—as in 100 percent stocks. Yes, it'll be volatile, and you won't always enjoy the ride. That's how the stock market works, but the long-term trend is up, which means that time will heal the wounds of a market downturn.

You could consider this sixteen-year guideline as too conservative. For one, it's the time period that has guaranteed you no losses. For an overwhelming majority of the time, ten years is plenty. Second, it was calculated by using only one group of stocks, albeit a broad one: US large company stocks. Including smaller company and foreign stocks should not require you to wait this long. However, international stocks don't have as long a data set. If you want to use ten years as your definition of long-term, I won't argue, but I think prudence dictates the extra years.

Illiquid investments

Remember return hurdles and opportunity costs? By now, I must sound like a broken record. But I'm not apologizing for it, because those two concepts are a huge part of capital allocation. Your opportunity cost is whatever else you could be using your capital for, and your return hurdle establishes when you should be attracted to a nontraditional investment.

One way investors have targeted higher returns than the typical stock and bond portfolio is through private illiquid investments. There can be different definitions and interpretations of investment illiquidity. For our purposes, we're going to simplify by explaining it as an investment that you cannot instantly sell for years. Anything with a publicly functioning market like publicly traded stocks and bonds is liquid.

The private investments you'll likely choose from are illiquid for around five to twelve years. You don't need me to tell you that that is a really long time. You're only going to allocate long-term money to these strategies. The extra return you should target should be a few percentage points more than our stock return hurdle of 9 percent—something like 12 percent to 13 percent. That has historically been the excess return available on investing in some private investment strategies, and anything less isn't worth the extensive lack of liquidity.

While there are many types of private investments, that amount of potential excess return is typically only available through private equity, private credit, and opportunistic real estate.

Type	Definition	Commitment
Private equity	Investing in private companies versus buying shares in publicly traded stocks	9–10 years
Private credit	Lending to private companies versus buying corporate bonds	5–6 years
Opportunistic real estate	Opportunistically purchasing properties that need significant investment and redevelopment to generate returns	9–10 years

Although I've included private credit on this list, in all likelihood, the return potential for private credit will rival what you can get in publicly traded stocks. Therefore, if you are investing long-term money, you may prefer the liquidity of stocks unless you target private credit for the diversification.

Investing in private, illiquid investments requires a different skill set and access to more information than traditional stock and bond investing. Private investments require deep sourcing expertise and resources to perform extensive due diligence, not just on the investment team and philosophy, but also on the private funds' legal structures and operational risks. There are a lot of terrible funds out there, and the difference between the good and the bad is significantly wider than with the publicly traded markets.

INTERMEDIATE BUCKET

By extension from the prior buckets, the intermediate bucket is for money you're going to need in the next four to fifteen years. When during that span you will need it and how much will determine your allocation. These variables mean these investments won't be as straightforward or precise. You're going to invest in stocks and bonds, but not more than 80 percent or less than 20 percent stocks. Anything over 80 percent will be too close to the volatility of an all-stock portfolio, and a portfolio with no stocks can be riskier than one with even a token amount.

I see two major scenarios for how and when you might need this bucket: You'll need all of it at some point or you'll need a certain percentage of it per year.

If you intend to cash out the entire bucket, I'd stick to the following ranges based on when you'll need it:

- 4–5 years: 20%–35% stocks and 65%–80% bonds
- 6–8 years: 35%–50% stocks and 50%–65% bonds
- 8–15 years: 50%–65% stocks and 35%–50% bonds

If you intend to have a steady withdrawal, I'd target the following asset allocation ranges for stocks with the rest being in bonds.

- Less than 4%: 65%–80% stocks
- 4%–5%: 50%–65% stocks
- 6%–7%: 35%–50% stocks
- More than 7%: 20%–35% stocks

Now that we have a sense of what asset allocation to choose depending on your situation, we should turn more specifically to the asset classes themselves. Stocks and bonds are very broad categories with many managers and products. The question is: how do we choose which ones to use?

INVESTMENT SELECTION

Once again, I can see this working only if we continue with KISS. Asset allocation is the primary driver of portfolio return, but we still need vehicles through which to implement that allocation. We've already determined that we're not going to pick individual stocks, so that leaves us two options—mutual funds and ETFs, which we discussed in the previous chapter. Skip picking stocks and instead invest in a basket of them managed by someone else. Easy, right? Well, not exactly. There are over ten thousand to choose from, and that number is growing.

Furthermore, some of what you would think would be good ways to choose aren't. Performance over the last three to five years relative to your peers is useless as a predictor of future performance. Top performers turn into awful performers more frequently than repeating that success. Rating systems like Morningstar's stars are ineffective, and that's according to Morningstar's own analysis. Preferred lists or magazine rankings haven't helped narrow the field either.

Instead, the KISS approach to investment selection has to be indexing. Indexing is investing in a fund (mutual or ETF) that tracks the performance of an investment index, like the S&P 500 for US stocks or the Bloomberg Barclays US Aggregate Bond Index for US investment grade bonds. There is still complexity with this approach, since there are plenty of indexes to choose from, but it simplifies the process enough: Find the right indexes and get index fund exposure to them for the asset classes we want in the portfolio.

Don't get me wrong. Indexing can be improved on, and it is not the best investment option out there. However, if you are going down this path of do-it-yourself investing, you need to minimize the possibility of costly mistakes. Indexing is a decent option with many advantages:

- Index funds are low-cost. The lower the cost, the more return you keep.

- Index funds are low-turnover vehicles that are tax-efficient. Tax efficiency also allows you to keep more of what you earn.

- They are tough to beat, so you're usually getting a strong performer within the categories you're investing in.

WHICH INDEXES?

Now that we've established our asset allocation approach and how we will select investments, we need to determine which indexes to choose for our asset allocation. Since we're investing in index funds, this finalizes the investment selection process as well. Let's deal with stocks first and then bonds.

STOCKS

The two main questions for stocks are how much to invest domestically versus internationally and then, within those baskets, which domestic and international index to select. Investors suffer from what is known as a home country bias, which means we anchor too much of our portfolios in our own country's stocks and ignore global investment opportunities. The global stock market is currently about 56 percent US stocks and 44 percent international stocks. Even a true global investor will have strong exposure to US stocks. The question for us as US investors is: how far into international investing do we go? The US market is broadly diversified, provides you with a good cross-section of industry and sector exposure, and provides international exposure, since a healthy portion of US company earnings are international, and foreign investing comes with different risks. Some counsel against owning any international stocks for this and other reasons. However, their numbers are shrinking, and studies have shown the benefits of owning international stocks. Beyond just diversification, they offer better long-term returns. A US-only portfolio offers lower risk but also lower returns than international investments.[24]

While there are reasons to be invested anywhere from 30 percent to 70 percent in international equities, the KISS framework should probably have us at a 70/30 US-international split, the level identified as adding return without adding risk, so that you don't need to determine how much risk you're willing to take for certain levels of potential excess return.

To implement that, find an index fund that tracks the performance of the Russell 3000 Index for US exposure. The Russell 3000 tracks the performance of the largest three thousand publicly traded companies in the United States. If you're a Vanguard acolyte and want to use their version, it is the Vanguard Total Stock Market Index Fund, which tracks a different but very similar US index. For international equities, find an index fund that tracks the FTSE Global All Cap ex US Index, which tracks the performance of close to six thousand international companies in more than forty-five countries.

BONDS

Whatever you do not own in stocks in your intermediate bucket should be invested in bonds. The percentages presented earlier were based on bonds providing stability—that is, reducing the portfolio's

---

24   Ferri, *All About Asset Allocation,* 70.

short-term volatility. For this reason, we won't be taking much risk with our bonds. Risk in bonds comes primarily in two forms: credit risk and interest rate risk. The first is the risk that you, as the bond-holder, will not be paid back. The second is the risk that bond prices will decline as interest rates rise. All things being equal, as interest rates increase, bond prices decrease. Picture a ten-year bond that pays you 4 percent and is valued at $100. If interest rates immediately rise and ten-year bonds are paying 5 percent, then your 4 percent bond will have to adjust downward in price to provide an equivalent return to the new market rate. The longer-term your bond is, the more sensitive it is to interest rate increases.

The Bloomberg Barclays US Aggregate Bond Index is a good one to track for bond exposure that meets our requirements. The bonds are investment grade, which means they are deemed good credit risks, and they are not long-term bonds subject to significant interest rate risk.

KEEP IT SIMPLE

The biggest risk of do-it-yourself investing is your own tendency to make poor investment timing decisions that can wreak havoc with long-term returns. Second to that is the reality that investing is a competitive marketplace that you do not want to venture into lightly. Although this method carries unnecessary risks, you can mitigate those risks somewhat by keeping it simple.

Within your investment buckets, establish asset allocation ranges to reduce risk and earn the returns that are prudent to target based on how long you can set the money aside. You can then implement that allocation through index funds in our continued quest to simplify this process and not set you up for failure by assuming skills you may not have. Finally, target specific indexes for stocks and bonds to minimize your risk.

KISS can serve you well if you can implement it, stick to it through market volatility no matter what, avoid the impulse to become greedy and more aggressive during market heydays, and resist the temptation to chase performance by buying hot funds or cutting losers too soon. Remember, the performance of your portfolio will likely not be primarily driven by how your investments perform but by how you, as an investor, behave.

CHAPTER 8

Common Investment Mistakes to Avoid

"In investing, what is comfortable is rarely profitable."
—Rob Arnott

N ow that we've walked through two distinct paths to accessing traditional investment, we need to highlight common investment mistakes that you will be exposed to regardless of whether you're working with an advisor or managing your own portfolio. Helping individual investors for the last twenty years has crystallized for me a core set of investment myths that, left unaddressed, lead to the timing mistakes we've discussed. They're presented here in the form of questions often asked by investors:

- What's wrong with getting out of the market now and jump-ing back in when things look better?

- Is now a safe time to invest?

- If a specific asset class is doing so much better than every-thing else, why not just put more money there?

- If some news source claims that now is a terrible time to invest in a specific asset class, why would you retain an investment in it?

GETTING IN AND OUT OF THE MARKET

Investing in stocks is hard. I'm not talking about skill and knowl-edge, which we already addressed. Owning stocks is hard. It makes us to want to do bad things, specifically bailing from the market during tough times and jumping back in when it's "better."

First, stock market volatility is unnerving. In the short term, markets move in different directions at fast speeds. One day's moves seem disconnected from the previous day's, and when markets decline, it's not just numbers on a screen. Real dollars seem lost for incomprehensible reasons, making it hard to remember that great long-term returns come from just standing pat.

Second, we're conditioned to act. Markets are declining and we're losing money. Shouldn't we do something? Isn't that what smart people, bold people do? Make a move to stop the bleeding. Even if it won't accomplish much, doesn't it feel reassuring to take action? Of course it does.

Third, there's always someone out there pushing the nonsense that successful market timing can be accomplished, and scaring us that things will get worse if we don't.

The recency bias is a behavior economists have identified that prevents us from making sound financial decisions. It occurs when we focus on recent events instead of the long term. In a down market, we forget the market's strong long-term returns and fixate on fears that the current decline is a new market paradigm to protect against. Instead of patience and discipline, we overreact to the moment by doing something that we instinctively know we shouldn't.

How do I know we know better? First, when someone brings up whether they should back out of the market, they invariably preface it by saying they know we can't time the market. They know it, but they can't stop themselves from asking. Second, when asked on an advisor's investment questionnaire how they'll react during market declines, people claim that they view them as buying opportunities—buying good investments at a cheaper price. What they actually do during those declines is quite different. It's the rare case when someone wants to become more aggressive.

The recency bias wreaks havoc by changing your view of the market and getting you to do things you know you shouldn't. Declines are a buying opportunity, versus a time to sell low. Stick to the discipline and knowledge you already have.

THERE'S NO POINT

You don't need the impossible to earn strong portfolio returns. The following three charts help illustrate why. The first one—time, diversification, and the volatility of returns—shows three portfolios:

- 100% US stocks
- 100% US bonds
- 50/50 split

Time, diversification and the volatility of returns

GTM – U.S. | 63

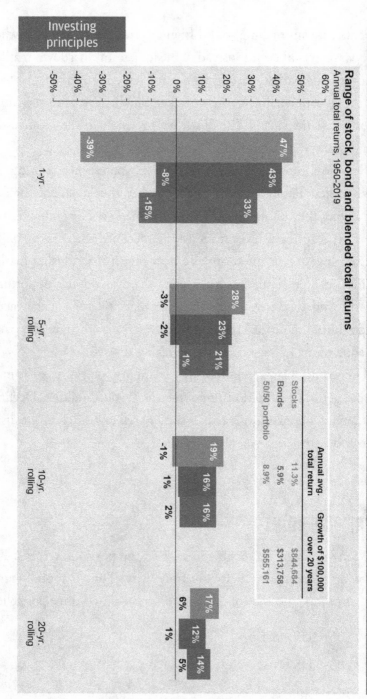

Investing principles

Range of stock, bond and blended total returns
Annual total returns, 1950–2019

	Annual avg. total return	Growth of $100,000 over 20 years
Stocks	11.3%	$844,684
Bonds	5.9%	$313,758
50/50 portfolio	8.9%	$555,161

1-yr.
47%
43%
33%
-8%
-15%
-39%

5-yr. rolling
28%
23%
21%
-3%
-2%
1%

10-yr. rolling
19%
16%
16%
-1%
1%
2%

20-yr. rolling
17%
14%
12%
6%
5%
1%

Source: Barclay's, Bloomberg, FactSet, Federal Reserve, Robert Shiller, Strategas/Ibbotson, J.P. Morgan Asset Management.

Focusing only on the portfolios with stocks in them—the lighter bars on the left—we see that the longer you are invested, the less downside risk there is to be worried about. Sure, in their worst year, stocks declined 39 percent, and the 50/50 portfolio declined 15 percent, but as you extend your time periods, those numbers improve. At five and ten years, the all-stock portfolio has modest losses (which is why you're bucketing if you're doing this yourself), and at fifteen years, the worst average annual return is 6 percent. These numbers differ a bit from the bucketing approach, since, here, the returns go back to 1950 instead of 1927.

The 50/50 portfolio was positive over all five-, ten-, and fifteen-year time periods.

If you've invested in the right asset allocation based on your time horizon, you shouldn't need market timing to protect your investments. They're protected already. The market provides great long-term returns. The only way to miss them is by overreacting to short-term volatility and abandoning your plan.

The second chart provides context about the large market declines people most worry about. The third chart shows that double-digit market declines are common—basically an annual occurrence—and the average intrayear decline is 13.8 percent. Note that this doesn't mean the market loses 13.8 percent per year, just that during the year, that size of drop occurs on average.

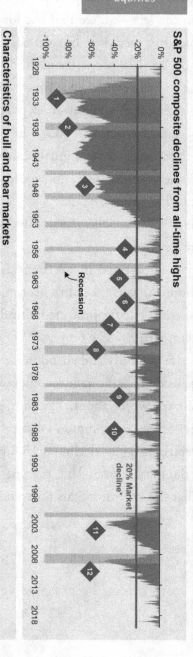

Bear markets and subsequent bull runs   GTM – U.S. | 14

Equities

S&P 500 composite declines from all-time highs

(Chart y-axis: 0%, -20%, -40%, -60%, -80%, -100%; x-axis: 1928, 1933, 1938, 1943, 1948, 1953, 1958, 1963, 1968, 1973, 1978, 1983, 1988, 1993, 1998, 2003, 2008, 2013, 2018)

Recession

20% Market decline*

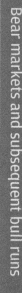

Characteristics of bull and bear markets

Market Corrections	Market peak	Bear markets Bear return*	Duration (months)¹	Macro environment Recession	Commodity spike	Aggressive Fed	Extreme valuations	Bull markets Bull begin date	Bull return	Duration (months)
1 Crash of 1929 - Excessive leverage, irrational exuberance	Sep 1929	-86%	32	◆				Jul 1926	152%	37
2 1937 Fed Tightening - Premature policy tightening	Mar 1937	-60%	61	◆				Mar 1935	129%	23
3 Post WWII Crash - Post-war demobilization, recession fears	May 1946	-30%	36	◆				Apr 1942	158%	49
4 Eisenhower Recession - Worldwide recession	Aug 1956	-22%	14	◆				Jun 1949	267%	85
5 Flash Crash of 1962 - Flash crash, Cuban Missile Crisis	Dec 1961	-28%	6					Oct 1960	39%	13
6 1966 Financial Crisis - Credit crunch	Feb 1966	-22%	7					Oct 1962	76%	39
7 Tech Crash of 1970 - Economic overheating, civil unrest	Nov 1968	-36%	17	◆		◆		Oct 1966	48%	25
8 Stagflation - OPEC oil embargo	Jan 1973	-48%	20	◆	◆	◆		May 1970	74%	31
9 Volcker Tightening - Whip Inflation Now	Nov 1980	-27%	20	◆	◆	◆		May 1978	62%	32
10 1987 Crash - Program trading, overheating markets	Aug 1987	-34%	3			◆	◆	Aug 1982	229%	60
11 Tech Bubble - Extreme valuations, .com boom/bust	Mar 2000	-49%	30	◆		◆	◆◆	Oct 1990	417%	113
12 Global Financial Crisis - Leverage/housing, Lehman collapse	Oct 2007	-57%	17	◆	◆		◆	Oct 2002	101%	60
Current Cycle	-	-	-					Mar 2009	378%	129
Averages	-	**-42%**	**22**					-	**164%**	**54**

Source: FactSet, NBER, Robert Shiller, Standard & Poor's, J.P. Morgan Asset Management.

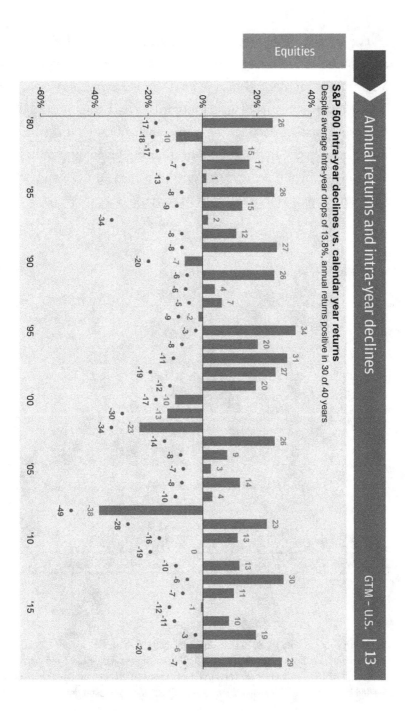

Equities

Annual returns and intra-year declines

GTM – U.S. | 13

S&P 500 intra-year declines vs. calendar year returns
Despite average intra-year drops of 13.8%, annual returns positive in 30 of 40 years

The dreaded 20 percent declines representative of a bear market, however, are probably less frequent and shorter than you think. We've had eight since World War II, and they average two years. They happen, and they can temporarily derail your portfolio, but most stock market declines don't turn into a bear, and the recovery from bears starts quickly. Proper positioning by owning only stocks with long-term money means you don't need to develop a crystal ball to avoid permanent losses in bear markets.

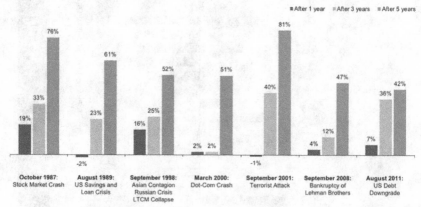

The Market's Response to Crisis
Performance of a Balanced Strategy: 60% Stocks, 40% Bonds
Cumulative Total Return

In US dollars.
Represents cumulative total returns of a balanced strategy invested on the first day of the following calendar month of the event noted. Balanced Strategy: 12% S&P 500 Index, 12% Dimensional US Large Cap Value Index, 6% Dow Jones US Select REIT Index, 6% Dimensional International Value Index, 6% Dimensional US Small Cap Index, 6% Dimensional US Small Cap Value Index, 3% Dimensional International Small Cap Index, 3% Dimensional International Small Cap Value Index, 2.4% Dimensional Emerging Markets Small Index, 1.8% Dimensional Emerging Markets Value Index, 1.8% Dimensional Emerging Markets Index, 10% Bloomberg Barclays Treasury Bond Index 1-5 Years, 10% FTSE World Government Bond Index 1-5 Years (hedged), 10% FTSE World Government Bond Index 1-3 Years (hedged), 10% ICE BofA 1-Year US Treasury Note Index. Assumes monthly rebalancing. For illustrative purposes only. S&P and Dow Jones data © 2019 S&P Dow Jones Indices LLC, a division of S&P Global. All rights reserved. ICE BofA index data © 2019 ICE Data Indices, LLC. FTSE fixed income indices © 2019 FTSE Fixed Income LLC. All rights reserved. Bloomberg Barclays data provided by Bloomberg. Dimensional indices use CRSP and Compustat data.
Indices are not available for direct investment. Their performance does not reflect the expenses associated with the management of an actual portfolio. Past performance is not a guarantee of future results. Not to be construed as investment advice. Returns of model portfolios are based on back-tested model allocation mixes designed with the benefit of hindsight and do not represent actual investment performance.

That you'll recover after these downturns is reflected well in the fourth chart. It shows the recovery over different time periods for a 60 stock/40 bond portfolio after five recent financial crises. Three years later, all was well except for one of them. Five years out, we were in the black across the board.

IS NOW A SAFE TIME TO INVEST?

By now, you've likely figured out how I'll answer these questions, since the concepts behind the answers overlap. Accordingly, we don't have to spill too much ink on this one. If you have allocated capital correctly by first paying off bad debts, setting aside enough cash for a rainy day, and hiring an advisor who did some planning for investing only long-term money in stocks (or you set up your own bucket approach the same way), then it's safe to invest that long-term money.

Most of the time, the market is up—about three-quarters of all years' market returns are positive. Saying the next twelve months won't be one of those times is a market timing call or a forecast. We don't do those and you know why. You also know that even if we invest before a downturn, we'll be fine before too long.

Put the money to work. Don't miss out on returns. You need to invest to make money. Keeping long-term money uninvested is an capital allocation mistake. Put the money where it is meant to be since the risks to getting in at the wrong time are small and the harm can be quickly overcome.

WHY DO WE OWN AN ASSET CLASS THAT IS STRUGGLING?

Some version of this question comes up a lot. You build a diversified portfolio with different asset classes or different types of investments within each asset class. Part of the idea is that having different sources of portfolio returns is beneficial. Those different sources provide diversification, so if one investment isn't doing well, maybe another one is. Smoother returns should make it easier to stick to the portfolio. Less volatility also leads to better long-term returns.

Consider this example. Portfolio A is $10,000 and earns the following returns:

Year	Return
1	20%
2	−10%
3	12%
4	−5%
5	10%

At the end of year 5, the $10,000 is $12,640, and the average annual return is 5.4 percent.

Portfolio B is $10,000 and earns a steady 4.9 percent per year, 0.5 percent less than portfolio A. This portfolio grows to $12,702—half a percent less per year but more money.

We can argue about me cherry-picking numbers to make a point (I did), and how realistic both return streams are (no clue), but I'm illustrating a mathematical point, and my math teachers delighted in telling me you can't argue with math.

You've set up your diversified portfolio, and what happens? Well, not to be too obnoxious about it, but the diversification works. Some investments do well, and some don't. Those that don't do well frustrate you, so you want to dump them and add more to the winners. You either ask your advisor if you should or, if you're managing your own money, do it yourself.

2004	2005	2006	2007	2008	2009	2010	2011	2012	2013	2014	2015	2016	2017	2018
33.9	34.5	36.0	39.8	8.8	79.0	28.1	9.4	18.6	38.8	32.0	5.4	21.3	37.8	2.1
33.2	25.2	32.6	8.2	6.6	49.4	26.9	3.4	18.6	32.4	13.7	4.5	12.0	32.1	1.9
26.0	13.8	25.0	6.3	4.7	28.5	22.9	2.3	17.1	27.2	4.9	1.4	11.6	21.8	1.5
18.3	4.9	18.4	5.9	-33.8	27.2	19.2	2.1	16.3	1.2	1.9	1.0	6.7	14.6	-4.2
10.9	4.6	15.8	5.5	-37.0	26.5	15.1	0.6	16.0	0.6	1.2	0.9	5.5	3.8	-4.4
2.7	3.1	4.3	5.3	-39.2	2.3	3.7	-4.2	2.1	0.3	0.2	0.2	1.5	1.1	-11.0
1.3	2.4	4.1	-1.6	-47.0	0.8	2.0	-13.6	0.9	-0.1	-1.8	-4.4	1.0	0.7	-14.2
0.8	1.3	3.8	-17.6	-53.2	0.2	0.8	-18.2	0.2	-2.3	-5.8	-14.6	0.8	0.6	-18.8

Legend:
- S&P 500 Index
- Russell 2000 Index
- Dow Jones US Select REIT Index
- Dimensional International Small Cap index
- MSCI Emerging Markets Index (gross div.)
- ICE BofA 1-Year US Treasury Note Index
- Bloomberg Barclays US Treasury Bond Index 1–5 Years
- FTSE World Government Bond Index 1–5 Years (hedged to USD)

This is a bad idea. Winners rotate, and abandoning one poor-performing investment to chase a winner is not what you want to do. Instead of buying low and selling high, you're doing the opposite. A poor-performing investment is cheaper than before—low. A strong-performing investment is more expensive than before—high. Why would you constantly make this swap? Patience is rewarded. Your laggards will become your winners and vice versa. Don't miss out on smoother returns by chasing performance.

THE NEWS IS BAD

Let me clarify something. This section isn't about the oft-expressed concern about whether now's the right time to invest given bad news in the world. For me, and most advisors, the answer is always the same:

- It's impossible to anticipate how markets are going to react to any news or event.
- It's impossible to time the markets even if you could make that anticipation.
- As long as you're investing the right way based on your time horizon, you'll be fine.
- Stock markets can move in the short term based on news, but in the long run, they're driven by the long-term performance of the underlying businesses.

Instead, this is a warning to protect yourself against something that seems like a good idea but isn't. This is a warning to protect yourself against a market timing temptation that arrives in the sheep's clothing of fake investment advice. Simply put: Markets discount, and the news reports. Getting that backwards is easy and can crush your portfolio. This scenario is also connected to the last question we addressed: Some asset class is getting killed, so why do we own it when this other one is doing much better? It's basically its sophisticated older cousin.

You own an investment—let's say it's an emerging markets stock fund. The fund is performing poorly, while your US stock investments are doing well. You want to dump the loser but know you shouldn't be so fickle. So you stick to your plan. Then you start reading. Articles in *The Economist, The Wall Street Journal,* and the like are talking about how bad the emerging markets are performing. They explain what's going on in those economies and markets that may be making their markets perform poorly. It's all bleak and ugly stuff leading to bleak and ugly returns, including pithy quotes about how bad things are.

Aha! You knew it. You have to get out of that investment now.

Or do you? This is a news article, not an investment analysis, despite the august publication it's in. A market is performing poorly and a respected media outlet is telling you about it. But they're telling you about more than just this market being down by a certain percentage, because that would be a boring and short article. They're also providing context by informing you about what's not going well and including some great quotes.

I hate most weather analogies—unless they're my own and I really need to make a point—but when the weather report tells you it's cold and wet outside, why it's cold and wet, and the precautions you should take to stay safe, warm, and dry, it doesn't mean they canceled spring. It's just what this raw winter day looks like. Reporters aren't investment analysts.

Major jargon alert: The markets are a discounting mechanism.

Markets discount, which means that market participants make investment decisions today about expected future returns. The news is about today; investing is about the future. That emerging markets investment that's been tanking—yes, it's had an ugly ride, but what will it do from here? Is this an attractive price to buy it, since the future earnings you are purchasing cost less? The US stock fund that's been on a tear—that's been a great investment until now—what'll happen to it next? Maybe it's still reasonably priced and will continue to do well, or maybe that dollar of earnings you are buying is now too expensive to expect a decent return. If it's in the news, it's already priced into the investments. Markets react quickly to information, and investing is a forward-looking endeavor.

Don't take the pessimistic or optimistic news report as much more than news, even when they include predictions that things will continue on the same path. The only certainty is change.

IT AIN'T EASY ALLOCATING GREEN

Investing is not easy. The daily fluctuations can make your head spin and create stress when attached to your dollars and cents. You can increase your odds for success with traditional portfolios, whether you do it yourself or—better—hire an advisor. Hopefully, in reviewing the questions here, you came away better equipped to handle market stress.

Jumping out during downturns and getting back in when things are safer sound great, except for the impossibility of doing so and that you must be invested in the market to earn its long-term returns. If you set up your portfolio allocation correctly based on your time horizon, it's always a safe time to invest, since you are not going to need to sell out of your long-term investments during market declines.

Market winners rotate, and chasing performance will have you constantly selling investments low to buy other ones high. Give your portfolio strategy time, since diversification means that not all of your holdings will be doing well simultaneously. Finally, news articles can be great sources of information, but they are not actionable market research. Stick to your plan!

CHAPTER 9

Real Estate Investing

"Every person who invests in well-selected real estate in a growing section of a prosperous community adopts the surest and safest method of becoming independent, for real estate is the basis of wealth."

—Theodore Roosevelt, US president (1901–09)

A s we learned in our discussion of evaluating traditional investments, return hurdles and opportunity costs should be baked into all of your capital allocation decisions—and that includes real estate. Long-term capital should seek the highest achievable returns, thus we're not talking about pursuing non-stock and bond investments for just diversification or to reduce risk. You can build a diversified portfolio of stocks and bonds, and you can reduce risk to yourself through the right asset allocation.

Real estate is a prominent example of a type of investment that people have used successfully to build wealth; however, you have to think about real estate investing differently than how you think about stocks and bonds. You must consider what role real estate should play in your portfolio, the different types of real estate investments, how to successfully invest in real estate on your own or through a manager, and some ways you can make your real estate investing more tax-efficient. But first, there are three real estate myths I want you to ignore in order to make stronger return hurdle decisions.

REAL ESTATE MYTHOLOGY

Real estate can be an excellent investment, but unfortunately, too many financial advisors ignore it, because it's not a traditional one they understand. This causes clients and prospective clients to worry about a conflict of interest with those advisors who are paid based on the assets they manage—the more the clients have in real estate, the less will be invested in their portfolios generating fees. That might be true for some advisors but not the good ones. Instead, this is a clash of belief systems. Most advisors believe in the traditional markets. They know that clients will do well long-term investing in stocks and bonds. They understand how to put market volatility in context, that volatility is an imperfect way of looking at what risk really is, and that much of their day job centers on this belief that stocks and bonds provide the best path to wealth creation.

At the same time, real estate carries with it a certain mythology that can make its advocates oversell its virtues, as exemplified by the quote beginning the chapter. The irony is that Teddy Roosevelt was a horrible manager of his own finances, so he's not exactly an investment authority, just another mythmaker. Instead of battling over which type of investment is better, let's instead focus on dispelling a few myths surrounding real estate, so you can choose to invest in it for the right reasons. Then, we'll highlight some excellent reasons why you should.

MYTH 1: BUY REAL ESTATE FOR PRICE APPRECIATION

Please don't invest in real estate because you think prices increase faster than stock prices. Real estate can build wealth but typically not primarily through price appreciation. Studies of long-term real estate returns show that historically real estate prices have not grown much faster than the rate of inflation. In a 2016 *New York Times* article, Robert J. Shiller, a Nobel Prize–winning economist who has studied and created ways to evaluate long-term asset class valuations and performance, including for real estate, wrote that, over the long run, "land and homes have actually been disappointing investments"[25] if you look at just prices. According to his data, home prices between 1915 and 2015 increased only 0.6 percent per year more than inflation.[26] During that same time period, the S&P 500 earned an annualized real return of 6.7 percent,[27] and 10-year Treasury bonds earned 1.8 percent real returns.[28]

---

25   Robert Shiller, "Why Land and Homes Actually Tend to Be Disappointing Investments," *The Upshot (blog)*, *The New York Times*, July 17, 2016, https://www.nytimes. com/2016/07/17/upshot/why-land-may-not-be-the-smartest-place-to-put-your-nest-egg. html.

26   Shiller, "Disappointing Investments."

27   "S&P 500 Return Calculator, with Dividend Reinvestments," *Don't Quit Your Day Job*, accessed November 1, 2019, https://dqydj.com/sp-500-periodic-reinvestment-calculator- dividends.

28   "Treasury Return Calculator, with Coupon Reinvestment," *Don't Quit Your Day Job*, accessed October 16, 2019, https://dqydj.com/treasury-return-calculator.

I can hear the protests now: *That doesn't make sense. My parents bought a home in 1985 and sold it last year for triple the price! Stocks never do that! Real estate is an awesome investment.* Well, tripling your money over thirty years is a 3.73 percent average annual return. That's not very impressive over three decades. During that time, the S&P 500 returned 11.1 percent per year, or 1,081 percent total—more than ten times the initial investment.[29]

MYTH 2: REAL ESTATE NEVER LOSES ITS VALUE

Stock market volatility stinks. Plunking most of your net worth into something that can decrease in value so quickly and sharply can be stressful. You're investing in businesses. How is it possible that their values can change so quickly? And when they do change for the worse, why all the bright red arrows on TV, and the noise and fake explanations that make it seem like those moves happened for a reason you should worry about?

Daily 1 percent moves aren't uncommon. We've already seen that the average intrayear decline is close to 14 percent with stocks. In the 2000s, we had two US market declines greater than 40 percent each. It's enough to make a lot of investors channel their inner Roberto Duran and say *no más*. This isn't theoretical. We've noticed it with younger investors whose first investment memories are of the tech wreck and credit crisis, and studies confirm. Even for money they won't need for at least ten years, Millennials scared by the lost decade of 2000–2010 are less likely than other generations to believe

---

29   "S&P 500 Return Calculator, with Dividend Reinvestments," *Don't Quit Your Day Job*, accessed November 1, 2019, https://dqydj.com/sp-500-periodic-reinvestment-calculator-dividends.

in stocks and have a stronger preference for other things, like real estate. They don't trust the stock market, and they're big believers in the myth that real estate never loses its value.

However, please don't let stock market volatility fool you into the idea that real estate values never decline. *I hate the market because I always lose money, but my house never goes down in price.* This is a whopper you hear a lot as an advisor. Real estate can lose value. Between 2005 and 2012, home prices declined by 43 percent,[30] nearly matching the 47 percent decline of stocks during the last bear market.

In the longer term, Shiller's data shows that national real estate price declines are not uncommon. While those decreases aren't always as pronounced as stock market ones, we've also seen that real estate price increases aren't as strong as stock price increases either.

The other difference between the two asset classes that feeds into this is painfully obvious but always bears repeating: Between 9:30 a.m. and 4:00 p.m. most weekdays, you can get a second-to-second update on the stock market's value. And as we've discussed, during those seconds, minutes, days, weeks, months, and even years, it can look like the stock market is a random spaghetti chart of unpredictable and potentially weak returns. If you treated the market like you do your house and only valued it whenever you were getting it prepped for sale, then you'd have a much different opinion on how volatile and risky the market is and you'd find it much easier to own stocks.

---

30   Aron Szapiro, "House of Cards: The Misunderstood Consumer Finance of Homeownership," Hello Wallet, November 2014, p. 1. Accessed on Rental Home Council website, https://www.rentalhomecouncil.org/wp-content/uploads/2017/07/HelloWallet-House-of-Cards.pdf.

MYTH 3: THEY'RE NOT BUILDING MORE LAND

Obviously, I know that the earth is not expanding. You can stop yourself from returning the book now and questioning my sanity. The myth here is that real estate is a great investment because we're not "making" any more land. But new land is developed or repurposed all the time, so this myth is too simplistic. If you're going to latch onto an idea like this, you should probably know how much land could still be developed in the United States. I personally have no idea, but I see miles and miles of undeveloped land whenever I drive around. If it were all built up, we'd have a huge oversupply of housing that would cause real estate prices to collapse.

Land doesn't have value because of the per-square-foot price of dirt. It has value when it's developed and used. And so, while we're not adding more land, we are making the land we have more accessible for development all the time. Whenever we do that, we are making more land economically useful, thereby creating competition for existing real estate. While we have the land we're going to have, we're nowhere near converting it all into something useful, so please don't get lazy with your analysis and invest in real estate over a myth.

REAL ESTATE'S ROLE IN YOUR PORTFOLIO

None of the preceding myth talk is intended to portray real estate as a bad investment. Done correctly and for the right reasons, it can be a great place to allocate capital. Let's discuss some good reasons to invest in real estate—namely, diversification and, more important, strong returns—then we can get into how to do it.

Real estate helps diversify a portfolio. The price of real estate won't always move in tandem with stocks and bonds, and as we've discussed, even if the real estate market is weaker, you won't know the exact impact on your property value second by second, since CNBC won't care to broadcast it to you. Prices are less volatile to begin with, although we know that's a mixed blessing, since it typically also leads to less price upside. Historically, real estate has had returns and volatility somewhere between an all-stock portfolio and an all-bond portfolio.

EXHIBIT 3: ANNUALIZED TOTAL RETURN COMPARISON (DECEMBER 1977–MARCH 2012)

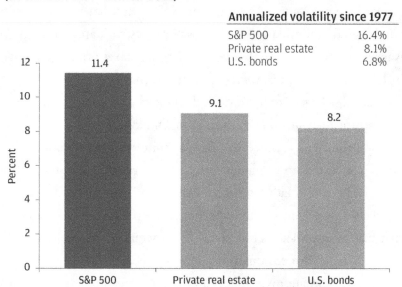

Annualized volatility since 1977	
S&P 500	16.4%
Private real estate	8.1%
U.S. bonds	6.8%

Source: NCREIF, Barclays Capital, Standard & Poor's, J.P. Morgan Asset Management.

S&P 500 Index for U.S. equities, Lehman Aggregate Bond Index for U.S. bonds and the NCREIF Property Index (unlevered) for U.S. private real estate. Quarterly returns are used to calculate annualized volatility for the S&P 500 and Lehman Agg. Since annual returns are used for real estate to de-smooth, volatility is calculated for the period from December 1977 through December 2011 for all three sectors.

While it didn't hold up particularly well in the Great Recession (2007–2009) when practically everything you could invest in got pummeled, in most other environments, when a stock-bond mix is negative, real estate is positive.

However, since you're either working with an advisor who can build an asset allocation appropriate for your time horizon or bucketing on your own, diversification for the sake of minimizing short-term volatility isn't a major concern. Therefore, pursuing it isn't enough of a reason to invest in real estate, even with decent return potential.

You might argue that rental income from your property can be a nice boost when the stock market isn't performing well. That's true, but we may not want to be overly impressed with that either, since in your capital accumulation and growth phases, you are not likely to want additional income that you have to pay taxes on; rather, you'll be looking for long-term, tax-efficient returns.

Instead, we want to focus on real estate when it provides competitive returns for your long-term money. Think back to our discussion of opportunity cost. Since you have a finite amount of capital, you need to allocate it to its highest potential return. In this instance, real estate is charting a path toward a 6 percent to 7 percent return, so you are likely costing yourself an opportunity to earn stronger returns with that money elsewhere. This means that I wouldn't get excited about a real estate investment unless it modeled out to a return exceeding 9 percent. Real estate investments are illiquid, meaning you can't easily access the capital you put into them, so it goes in your long-term bucket, which—remember—we set at a return hurdle of 9 percent by tying it to an expected long-term stock market return.

What types of real estate investments does that mean? Broadly speaking, there are two types you can make: those targeting income and those targeting total return. Income investing is accessible typically through decent properties that don't constantly need repair and for which you can charge healthy rent that covers your costs. These should be properties that are purchased either outright or with small mortgages that allow you to maximize your cash flow. Total return investing is similar in many ways, but you're borrowing more (higher leverage), which means your initial investment amount is lower. This leads to a higher potential total return. Total return investing can also include properties that you can improve cost-effectively to drive up the value or rents received to generate an outsized return compared to the pure income play.

HOW TO INVEST IN REAL ESTATE

Similar to our thoughts on traditional portfolio investing, we'll look at how to select real estate investments in two ways: how to do it yourself as an investor and how to do it through someone else's professional fund.

On your own, it's crucial to know how to find rental properties, how to value a property to see if it's a good investment, and how to build models with the proper assumptions to determine whether to proceed. From there, you need to understand why you may decide to invest through a fund instead and how to find one. Finally, you may be able to claim tax benefits through depreciation and tax-free exchanges.

DIY RENTAL PROPERTIES

Like other investments, rental properties must be purchased with a keen eye on price. You want value for the money you're spending by paying an attractive price for property that will generate sufficient cash flow to be highly profitable. The exact return you should target can be relative, even though I've shared my personal views about this already. For me, real estate is more of a hassle than investing in stocks and bonds, so I wouldn't do it unless I was targeting better returns than I could earn in my portfolio. However, people who aren't comfortable investing in stocks might target a lower return hurdle than I would. For them, real estate can be attractive if it has returns comparable to the stock market or has return potential stronger than bonds. This isn't optimal capital allocation, but not everything we do can be optimal.

With your return hurdle, the analysis begins. Step one is to sift through potential properties to determine which are worth more analysis. One way to do a quick screen on a property is through something known as the gross rent multiplier (GRM). You take the property's price (including up-front improvement costs) and divide it by its gross annual rent (meaning the rent you receive without considering any associated property expenses). The lower the number, the better, like when you're looking at price-to-earnings (P/E) ratios with stocks. A P/E ratio divides the price of the stock by the per-share earnings. The GRM is best used to compare similar properties, and while there's no perfectly attractive GRM when you're not comparing properties, most of the literature suggests a good target GRM is between eight and twelve.

Some investors focus on the capitalization (or cap) rate, so we should discuss it here. It's another helpful approach. The cap rate is the net operating income you can expect a property to generate as a percentage of its price. You take the total income received net of any expenses and divide that number by the property value. Most people target a cap rate of 5 percent or higher. Financing costs such as your mortgage aren't considered expense costs.

Cap rates can be informative, but similar to the GRM, you shouldn't use them to make final decisions. Properties can model out better or worse than both of these ratios would lead you to believe. A good cap rate is likely a great thing, but I wouldn't throw out a property with a bad one without running further numbers.

Let's say you put 20 percent to 30 percent down on a rental property, borrow the rest, and charge rent that covers your bills and a realistic maintenance budget. Fortunately, your property increases in value, your renters continue to cover your costs, and you implement regular rent increases while your mortgage payment remains fixed. This combination of factors provides you with a strong total return. To achieve this, you need to find properties that generate positive cash flow from day one and then see if they model out.

Here's how: First, run your initial screens per the discussion above. For income, determine the expected rent. If you're buying the property from the current landlord, you can request this data and verify it through Schedule E of their tax return. You could also use the online tool Rentometer or ask a good real estate agent. Model a vacancy rate, since it would be foolish to assume 100 percent rentability. A rate of 90 percent seems more reasonable. Then model a rent increase. To be conservative, I typically use 3 percent, so I am not assuming rent increases greater than long-term inflation. However, the fact that rent should increase at least with the rate of inflation is a great benefit of real estate over bonds. Not only is your income staying up with purchasing power, but in times of higher inflation, you should be able to charge higher rent to keep the property as attractive as it was when you first modeled it out.

For expenses, include property taxes, insurance, maintenance and repairs, financing costs, property management costs, utilities a landlord would cover, and condo or homeowners' association fees.

For all expenses except your mortgage, I would assume a 3 percent annual increase. Figuring out the initial maintenance and repair costs is a guess, so use 1.5 percent a year of the property's value. Be realistic and conservative with your rent and expense assumptions to avoid a disappointing investment. If you assume property value grows at the rate of inflation based on our myth discussion above, you have all the input needed for your model. Again, you will want to see that you have positive cash flow from the outset after factoring in vacancies and an improvement budget.

Next, calculate the total expected profit over the investment's life. For example, assume you purchased a property with a thirty-year mortgage. When the mortgage is paid off, your profit would be the value of the home, minus your initial down payment, plus the aggregate surplus rents over the thirty years (you can assume some rate of return on the surplus rents with the assumption that you set the dollars aside in something that was earning money).

Translate that total profit into an annual rate of return and compare it to what your capital allocation hurdle was for making this investment. Pull the trigger or pass based on the numbers.

Here's a detailed example to help you create the model I outlined earlier. You have purchased a property for $250,000 with a down payment of 25 percent ($62,500). The total annual mortgage cost was $11,400. Note that when you are considering investment property, you have to model a mortgage rate that is higher than what you see quoted for purchases of primary residences because investment property mortgage rates are higher. Your first year's costs are the mortgage of $11,400, various expenses to run the property (including modeling that it will be vacant 10 percent of the time), and a maintenance reserve of 1.5 percent per year that starts at $4,500. The first year of rent assuming full occupancy is $43,000, but you factor that rent and nonmortgage costs increase by 3 percent. Property value increases by 3 percent. In the first year, the property has a surplus cash flow of $5,283.

If we stop here, we can see that the property's GRM is not that attractive. It's just under six, but again, this is a tool to compare properties to each other, not to make final decisions. The cap rate is 6.6 percent, which is considered attractive.

Thirty years from now, the property's appreciation is $339,141, which is the purchase price of $250,000 grown by 3 percent per year until it reached $589,141, minus the purchase price. The profit is $1,014,009, which is the value of the home that you now own outright, and the aggregate surplus rent you have received after recouping your initial down payment—$424,868. Your return is your profit over the initial investment of $62,500. It equals 9.73 percent per year.

Does that exceed your initial return hurdle? If so, make an offer! If it does not, then consider the opportunity cost and live to fight another day with the capital you have. This property does exceed our 9 percent hurdle by 0.73 percent, which, compounded over time, is a substantial difference. I'd likely pursue it if I had the capital to do so.

REAL ESTATE INVESTING THROUGH A FUND

Of course, real estate is similar to investing in a traditional portfolio in that you may decide to invest through professionals. I'm not talking about a team that includes a good real estate agent, real estate lawyer, and mortgage broker; those are essential even as a do-it-yourself landlord. Their combined expertise will be invaluable. Instead, I mean investing in real estate through a professionally managed fund.

A good fund saves you time and provides diversification since you may not have the means, time, and patience to build a portfolio of dissimilar properties. Of course, it comes with a cost—fees for professional management, in particular—but fees are really only an issue if you're not getting value for them.

Let's identify some of the ways to best select a professional real estate fund for investing. At the risk of stating the obvious, this is not an exhaustive list, but here are several factors to consider in your search.

THE STRATEGY

It's a basic starting point, but the first thing you should know is what strategy the fund is pursuing. We've already discussed targeting total return versus income. In industry terms, funds targeting income are usually referred to as *core real estate funds*. You're not looking for those. Instead, target funds called *core plus*, *value-added*, or *opportunistic*.

Core plus is a strategy that targets more than just a steady stream of income, although these funds seek to provide that as well. Through modest investments and property improvements, the real estate also has growth potential, thus enhancing the return you can receive.

Value-added properties are not usually producing income now but have high growth potential and more risk since they require fixing lots of issues to make them good investments.

Opportunistic investment takes it a step further and targets larger projects that require more time and capital to work out.

THE PEOPLE

You will want to know who is running the show, how deep the team is, how many years of experience they have, what their capabilities are, and whether there are any ethical red flags. Find this last piece by asking for a disclosure on any civil, criminal, or regulatory actions against the fund's managers. If they're registered with the SEC or a state, request their Form ADV filing. It will contain information on the firm and any required disclosures.

THE COMMITMENT

It's a good sign when the firm's own personnel and investment professionals are invested in the funds they manage. Ask them about this and get specifics. A token investment so they can say they're invested is not what you're looking for, but if a large portion of their staff is heavily invested, that's a good sign.

THE CONTRACT

What are the fees, and why does the fund manager consider them competitive? Are there investment minimums, and if so, how much? You'll also want to ask about liquidity options, so you know when you can get your money back.

THE KNOWLEDGE

Beyond learning what their strategy is, find out how that strategy is implemented, why the manager thinks they can accomplish their goals, and what they consider their competitive advantage in this space. How do they find the opportunities to invest in, and what type of diversification are they targeting? Try and back up their assertions by reviewing their actual track record and performance history. Was their track record achieved when they ran a smaller fund that was easier to manage or under the same conditions as their current business? If it's a new fund without a track record, consider passing unless they can demonstrate proven expertise somewhere else that they are bringing to this new venture.

REFERENCES

Finally, ask for several references to other clients in a situation similar to yours, so you can assess their experience with the fund.

REAL ESTATE TAX EFFICIENCY

The returns available to you as a landlord can be earned tax-efficiently. Let's review the components of total return included in our model—value increases, mortgage reduction, and rent—to see why.

The property's annual price appreciation isn't taxable every year. Instead, the gains are deferred until you sell the property. The annual increase in equity as your mortgage is paid down isn't taxable to you either. Your net worth is increasing, but no income is being realized as it does. While rent is taxable income, you can deduct expenses of the property against it to reduce the amount of realized income you will be taxed on. For example, in our model, we had rental income of $43,000 that, absent any adjustments on Schedule E when you complete your tax returns, would flow through as taxable income. However, on the same sheet, we show costs of $21,817.

Line item	Cost
Condo fees	$8,000
Management fees	$4,000
Taxes	$3,517
Insurance	$2,000
Vacancy costs	$4,300
Total	$21,817

Those costs reduce your taxable income dollar for dollar from $43,000 to $21,183. Your mortgage interest, which is another cost not showing up here, is also deductible. The amount of interest you pay varies annually with a mortgage, but over the life of the loan modeled here, there would be $134,755 in interest payments that would reduce your taxable income.

DEPRECIATION

There is one other cost you can use to reduce your annual taxable income—depreciation. Depreciation is an annual cost you do not see but is nevertheless quite real. Per the IRS, "depreciation is an annual income tax deduction that allows you to recover the cost or other basis of certain property over the time you use the property. It is an allowance for the wear and tear, deterioration, or obsolescence of the property."[31] The IRS lets you deduct an annual depreciation expense for residential real estate under a schedule of 27.5 years. You can depreciate the home but not the land, so let's say the land for

---

31   *Publication 946: How to Depreciate Property*, Internal Revenue Service, 2018. Web.

the home in our model is $15,000 and the home is $235,000. You would receive an annual deprecation deduction of $7,727, shrinking your realized taxable income even further. As a side note, this is something to bear in mind as you consider how much in maintenance costs to build into your model. If the IRS is giving you a tax break under the theory that your property is going to deteriorate, don't make lofty assumptions that it will not. Depreciation wouldn't be deductible if it wasn't a legitimate cost.

This is tax deferral, not tax avoidance. When you sell the property, your price appreciation will be taxed as a capital gain (although any improvements you made to the house that weren't considered annual repair or maintenance expenses will be added to your cost basis to reduce your tax bill), and the depreciation will be taxed to you at a special tax rate through what the IRS calls *depreciation recapture*. As a reminder, capital gains are usually taxed at 15 percent or 20 percent. The depreciation recapture tax rate is 25 percent, higher than capital gains tax rates but likely lower than your marginal federal income tax rate.

The way this works in practice can be illustrated through the following example. You purchase a home for $100,000. You depreciate it over the years by $25,000. You sell it for $130,000. The $30,000 difference between the sales price and the purchase price is taxed as a capital gain. The $25,000 that was depreciated is taxed at the special 25 percent rate.

OUTRIGHT TAX DEFERRAL

It's important to end this chapter on real estate with a brief note on 1031 exchanges. These are complicated, so we do not need to get into every aspect of them. However, you can delay paying the tax on a real estate gain if you reinvest the proceeds in something similar. The exchange can be a simple swap of one property for another, and it can include cash and debt. These transactions can get quite complex, particularly when you go beyond exchanging one property for another, because the IRS also allows deferred exchanges and reverse exchanges. You have forty-five days from the date you sell a property to identify a specific new property that you would like to exchange into and 180 days (or the due date to file your next tax return) to complete the exchange.

INVEST FOR THE RIGHT REASONS

You should definitely consider real estate as a capital allocation option as you create your investment plan. The best capital allocators consider opportunity cost and target only competitive rates of return exceeding their return hurdles before allocating anywhere. Do the same with real estate. Invest in it for the right reasons, mainly because it's the best place to make returns, and ignore the mythology that has built up around it. Respect the difficulty of doing any type of investing yourself and, at the very least, have a great real estate team around you. You should also consider working with an advisor or finding the right real estate investment fund for your situation using the due diligence tips provided here. Make sure you are realistic with your assumptions, and remember and understand the tax benefits potentially available to you with real estate that are not available with other investments.

PART 3

Protecting Your Capital

"Everyone has a plan until they get punched in the mouth."

—Mike Tyson

What financial planning steps should you take to protect you and your family in the event your earnings potential and capital allocation journey are interrupted by death or disability? The young and successful ignore this too often. Perhaps it's a sense of invincibility, perhaps a lack of awareness of the risks and solutions. Maybe it's just an unwillingness to part with hard-earned capital to pay for protection or professional advice. Whatever the reason, you are failing as a capital allocator if these bases remain uncovered.

No matter how talented you are as a capital allocator, it'll take time to build your initial capital, develop a plan, and make it work. It's a long-term and continuous journey. Whether you start a business, invest in rental properties, create an investment portfolio, or pursue another path, you won't get rich overnight. Compounding is a lengthy process.

To provide you and your family protection if that process is interrupted by your untimely disability or death, start with disability insurance. The odds of disability are higher than you realize, and you should consider options to replace your lost income and capital if needed. These options include disability-related estate planning documents necessary to protect yourself.

Next, you should consider life insurance and estate planning documents to protect your family and assets in the event of your death. There are many different types of life insurance, so you should determine the amount you need and why. Review the pros and cons of different policies and follow best practices to be presented when purchasing one. For estate planning, you need to know which documents are necessary, how they can help with your planning, and what to consider in developing your own estate plan.

Finally, you need to look at protecting your capital from yourself. Bad investment decision-making can be the biggest impediment to your long-term success. You will constantly be tempted to deviate from your plan, you will constantly be fearful that you must react to market moves or headlines, and you will constantly be better off ignoring those temptations.

CHAPTER 10

Protecting against Disability

"Expect the best, prepare for the worst."
—Muhammad Ali Jinnah

Protecting yourself, your family, and your capital allocation plan in the event you suffer a terrible setback is important to ensure financial security for everyone. The right planning can help maintain your lifestyle if you can't earn income and protect your investments from having to be sold off quickly at unattractive prices to provide cash for basic needs.

Early in your career, your largest asset is your future human capital. The money you will earn trumps everything else until you have earned, saved, and invested. A twenty-five-year-old who earns $100,000 in their first year of work and gets raises of 3 percent per year until sixty-five will earn $7,866,330 during their career. (Of course, very few twenty-five-year-olds will be starting their career with that amount of money in the bank.) At thirty-five, they will have $6,585,550 in future earnings left. At forty-five, $4,998,681, and even at fifty-five with just ten working years left, they have $2,866,062 in future earnings. Time and continued career success will convert those potential dollars into real money unless you're disabled (or die) along the way. You need to pair your hopeful wealth creation plans with a strategy to protect yourself if things go wrong.

DISABILITY HAPPENS

According to the US Census Bureau, 16.6 percent of people between the ages of twenty-one and sixty-four in the United States had a disability in 2010, and 11.4 percent of Americans, or nearly 70 percent of disabled Americans, had a severe disability. This is the relevant age group, because we're focusing on your working career. Severe disabilities include such things as these:

- Being deaf or blind
- Being unable to perform one or more functional activities
- Needing a wheelchair, a cane, crutches, or a walker
- Needing assistance to perform one or more activities of daily living: getting around inside the home, getting in or out of bed or a chair, bathing, dressing, eating, or using the toilet
- Needing assistance to perform instrumental activities of daily living: going outside the home, managing money and bills, preparing meals, doing light housework, taking prescription medicines, or using the phone

- Having difficulty finding a job or remaining employed
- Being diagnosed with Alzheimer's disease, dementia, or senility

These are all serious conditions that limit your ability to earn money. You must protect yourself and your family from this risk. The protection comes in two forms: You must protect your unearned income through disability insurance, and you must protect your plans through estate planning.

DISABILITY INSURANCE

Disability insurance pays you money when you're disabled and can't work. Your financial plan should guide the amount of disability insurance coverage you will need if you're unable to work. It will replace the income needed to make ends meet and may even allow you to save enough for your long-term goals. There are three main avenues of disability insurance coverage: government programs, work plans, and private coverage.

Government programs include workers' compensation and Social Security Disability Insurance (SSDI). Workers' compensation covers you if you're injured on the job. It's important protection for certain professions, but most professionals are not at risk of job site injuries or illnesses. The overwhelming majority of disabilities occur off the job, and SSDI is quite difficult to qualify for and provides meager benefits.

A work-sponsored group plan is free to you, but the benefits are taxable because the employer paid the premium (unless the employer sets it up so that you're taxed on the premium payments they're making for you). Private coverage will generate tax-free income since you paid the premium, but you should consider the after-tax amount of the work benefit to ensure you have sufficient coverage. Other things to consider when purchasing a private policy are the definition of disability, the type of disability covered, the waiting period, the length of coverage, and inflation.

Pay attention to how coverage plans, work or private, define disability. Some policies cover you if you are unable to perform any occupation, while some will cover you only if you cannot perform your own occupation. A variation is that some will cover your own occupation for a time and then switch over to any occupation. Consider only the own occupation benefits that you receive through your work policy when assessing your coverage. You don't want to be forced to take a job you don't want or one that will be difficult based on your situation because you wouldn't be covered otherwise.

Look for policies that cover partial and not just total disability and that provide residual benefits (benefits for loss of income if you are able to work but not make as much as you used to).

A waiting period in disability insurance functions like a deductible. You decide how long to wait before receiving benefits once you are eligible. The typical periods range from thirty days to a year. Obviously, the longer the waiting period, the cheaper the premium. You should analyze the cost savings for longer periods versus the disability benefits forgone, and factor in your liquid savings and work coverage that will provide help during the waiting period.

The length of coverage is how long disability payments will last. Most people cover themselves for their working years—that is, until a normal retirement age of sixty-five. However, cheaper, shorter periods are available if that is all your financial plan requires.

Finally, target policies that provide a benefit increase every year through an inflation or cost-of-living adjustment rider. That way, your benefit can keep pace with inflation rather than you losing a certain amount of purchasing power each year.

Some policies include a feature that allows you to buy additional coverage without having to go through underwriting again so that your target benefit can keep pace with your growing career income.

Many financial planners will tell you that one of the hardest recommendations to get clients to agree with is purchasing their own disability insurance policies. That's certainly been my experience. Sure, you probably won't get disabled, but as we saw earlier, it's a realistic possibility. If it happens, the framework we've discussed should protect you.

Understanding the major items to consider when purchasing coverage, along with the help of an experienced professional, can take you through the coverage process successfully. Assess your work coverage, understand the benefits and gaps, and then use the pointers above to make a smart purchase of any supplemental coverage.

ESTATE PLANNING

You should also protect yourself and your family by having an updated estate plan. Estate plans protect against incapacity, as well as death. The inability to handle your own affairs can be planned for so that the courts don't determine who will make decisions for you. Those legal proceedings can be costly, time-consuming, fraught with family friction, and potentially embarrassing—or, at least, less private than you'd prefer. It's better to handle potential incapacity by documenting your preferences from the outset. This comes down to two key things: Who will handle your finances and who will make health-care decisions for you?

POWER OF ATTORNEY

A power of attorney document names someone to make financial decisions for you. You list what powers you want your agent to have. A good estate planning attorney can walk you through those potential powers and recommend the ones to include based on your situation. You should also name a successor to your agent in case the person you appointed is unable or unwilling to act.

Powers of attorney can be durable or springing. A durable document is in effect from the moment you sign it. Springing documents come into effect only when you are incapacitated. That seems like the way to go, since you may not want someone to have authority over your finances until you are unable to handle them yourself. However, most estate planning attorneys recommend durable powers for the simple reason that the agent appointed in a springing power can act on your behalf only after proving your incapacity to the court. This somewhat defeats the purpose of advanced planning.

REVOCABLE TRUST

A revocable trust is an estate planning document that you can transfer your assets into while you're living, and it governs how those assets pass after your death. You will likely be the initial trustee, and there are no practical differences between the assets being in your name or being in the name of your revocable trust while you are alive and well. But if you become disabled, a successor trustee could handle your financial affairs that involve the assets owned by your revocable trust.

HEALTH-CARE PROXY

A health-care proxy is a document naming an agent to make health-care decisions on your behalf in the event you cannot. Naming this person in advance eliminates the potentially costly and difficult battles between family members about who is entitled to make these decisions for you at a time of emotional strain. Here, again, you should name a successor to your original agent. You can also include language governing your preferences where there is no hope for recovery.

Estate planning is great for many reasons. In terms of protecting against disability, the right estate planning documents make your life and the lives of those you love easier if you're disabled by having you appoint the right people to make financial and health-care decisions for you. The alternative to this type of planning too often involves financial harm to the family and costly court intervention to figure these things out during stressful times.

WISHFUL THINKING

All the wishful thinking in the world does not minimize the possibility that you could become disabled at some point in your career. Instead of ignoring the possibility as many young capital allocators do, pursue the two-pronged strategy discussed here. Get disability insurance to replace lost income and implement an estate plan to minimize the financial disruptions caused by a severe accident or serious illness.

CHAPTER 11

Protecting Your Loved Ones and Your Future

"A man's dying is more his survivor's affair than his own."

—Thomas Mann

I n the late 1700s, people in Great Britain could gamble with life insurance by taking out a policy on someone they weren't connected to and profiting when that person died. It seems perverse because it is, and a British Act of Parliament ended this practice by creating the rules around what we now call *insurable interest*. These rules made life insurance available only to those who would suffer financially from the loss of the person being insured. You shouldn't profit when a random person dies. Conversely, you should have life insurance to provide for those who depend on you financially.

Life insurance is a complicated topic. First, you must figure out how much life insurance you need. There are different methods to assess this, but we can cut through to a more practical framework. Next, you must consider what type of life insurance to buy. We'll review the tax rules that add to life insurance's appeal and discuss best practices for how to improve on these general recommendations. Finally, you'll need certain estate planning documents beyond the ones discussed in the previous chapter to protect your family and plans from your death.

YOUR MAGIC NUMBER

Google *How much life insurance do I need?* and you'll find numerous calculators, articles, and sponsored ads for companies that would love to sell you a policy. When I used the first four calculators that showed up in the results to create a needs analysis for a hypothetical young family, I received a wide range of recommendations. That's because there are a variety of textbook ways to calculate your life insurance need and many assumptions that go into these calculations. We could try and master them and create a perfect answer in an imperfect arena, or we could focus on the bigger picture: You should replace enough of your unconverted human capital to ensure your family's finances will be fine without you.

Open that financial plan you hopefully created to guide your financial planning and investment decisions. Now, delete your future income and adjust your family's spending down to account for the fact that you're not around. Then figure out what other adjustments to make and start plugging hypothetical insurance proceeds into your brokerage account until the plan works again. The case study below illustrates how this can work in practice.

HOW MUCH LIFE INSURANCE? A MARRIED COUPLE

The husband is fifty and makes $180,000 per year. The wife is forty-eight and makes $40,000 per year. They spend $130,000 per year and antici-pate needing close to this in retirement. Their current portfolio is $1.2 million, and they have no life insurance. They have a decent financial plan, because they both plan on working for eighteen more years.

Assuming the husband passed away this year and his wife contin-ued to earn the same income but cut her spending by 25 percent, her assets would last her for only eighteen more years (until she's sixty-five). Adding $1.5 million to her portfolio through a hypothetical life insurance policy allows her assets to last her until the age of ninety-six. Therefore, the husband should take out a $1.5 million life insurance policy. Based on their plan, it should be kept in place until his retirement. Based on the same type of analysis, the wife should take out a $250,000 policy and keep it for at least ten years.

CHOOSING A POLICY TYPE

Life insurance comes in many forms, but the two main categories are temporary and permanent policies. Temporary policies are known as *term* policies, since they provide insurance for a term of years. There are different types of permanent policies, with *whole life* being the most well known.

Financial planners typically recommend term insurance in situ-ations like the case study above. Terms can be ten, twenty, or thirty years, or more. The longer the term, the more expensive the cover-age, but it's cheap insurance overall, since there's little likelihood of dying within the term selected. Once the term is up, you no longer have coverage, and the insurance company keeps your premiums. (Term policies can be extended on an annual renewal basis, but the premium jumps are dramatic, so let's just focus on how the policies work for the terms they're designed for.)

Hopefully, you see the attractiveness of these policies based on our work together so far. You have a capital allocation plan. It'll work over time because you are converting human capital into financial capital and allocating it well. But premature death can derail this, so you effectively rent a life insurance policy from a carrier. It's cheap and it'll cover you until you've converted enough human capital to no longer need it.

For most situations, term policies work well. They fit our framework and provide the necessary protection. That does not mean you should run and hide or freak out any time an insurance person tries to explain the benefits of permanent coverage. As we've seen, the best capital allocators are dynamic, flexible, and not locked into any preconceived notions or rules of thumb. You understand return hurdles now. You know not to get involved in anything you don't understand. If a different form of life insurance is presented to you, evaluate it as an investment and see if it fits into your capital allocation plan. A good agent can run internal rate of return illustrations, and a good financial planner will make sure the assumptions are reasonable.

Consider buying larger amounts of life insurance earlier if you are likely to need more future coverage. Let's say you are newly married with one child and have a small mortgage, but you are expecting more kids and a bigger home later. Consider purchasing more coverage now versus adding it in the future. Insurance becomes more costly as you age, and you may develop health issues that will make you less insurable.

Work policies are great ways to get cheap life insurance, but you typically lose them when you change jobs. I recommend not having all of your life insurance be work policies in case you have to replace all of that coverage at expensive rates later.

Replacing human capital is not your only life insurance need. If your spouse does not work, they should still be insured to cover things like childcare. You may even want to consider a larger amount so that you can take some time with your family away from work in the event of a tragic loss.

One final advantage of life insurance is that your beneficiaries will receive the death benefit income tax free, and if it is set up correctly, estate tax free.

ESTATE PLANNING

Once your life insurance coverage is squared away, you need to complete the set of estate planning documents we started discussing in the previous chapter. This may consist of getting a will, a will and a trust, or a will, a trust, and an additional life insurance trust to put a plan in place for handling assets after you're gone.

Most people procrastinate with getting their plan done, but you're not going to. You've come way too far to leave something so fundamental and basic undone. The bad news—beyond how careless this is—is that you already have an estate plan, even if you didn't create it. States have laws on their books, called the *laws of intestacy*, to figure out where people's assets will go if they die without a will. Intestacy laws differ across the states, but they can lead to strange and undesirable outcomes. For example, if you have living parents but no children, your surviving spouse may not inherit all of your assets. If you have children from multiple marriages, the split probably won't be what you intended either. So get your own plan instead of the arbitrary one set up by your state. This will also prevent any family skirmishes and court battles around what your wishes would have been had you taken care of this project.

A will allows you to appoint a guardian to care for your minor children in the event both parents have passed. You also name a personal representative to temporarily handle your finances and transition your assets.

Trusts provide for financial management so your spouse and minor children do not inherit large sums of money they may not be equipped to manage. Without a trust, your children will stand to inherit your assets at the age of eighteen or twenty-one (depending on the state) outright. Setting up a trust protects your privacy as well, since the details of it are not public record like your will would be.

Trusts can protect spendthrift heirs from themselves and creditors. When you create a trust, you appoint a trustee who has the legal obligation to administer it prudently according to the wishes laid out in your documents. If the trust's beneficiary is not the trustee and does not have unfettered access to the funds, the trust can be established so that its assets are not reachable by creditors or an irresponsible beneficiary.

An estate plan can help you save your family estate taxes. As you may be aware, the amount you can leave to your heirs (or give away during your life) without your estate having to pay a tax has been gradually increasing. It now stands at $11.2 million per person, or $22.4 million for a married couple. If you've gotten to the point financially where you need to worry about a federal estate tax, I thank you for reading up to this point and really have nothing else to add. However, if you live in one of the twenty-one states that have an estate or inheritance tax, an estate plan can help you take advantage of some of the techniques each one of those states allows to either save on your estate tax or defer it to the surviving spouse's passing.

This discussion is not about your becoming an estate planning expert but rather about making sure you understand the need for such planning and illustrating what can be accomplished. Your estate plan's actual structure depends on your situation and the advice you receive. Your role is to think about who should get what under what circumstances: If you're not married and have no children, where do you want the money to go? If you're married with no kids, do you want it to go to your surviving spouse and then someone else? If you're married with kids, maybe it goes to your spouse and then to take care of the kids? How much do the kids get and when? If you're in a second marriage, how much should you leave to your surviving spouse and then your children from the previous marriage? And at what ages should they get the funds? An estate planning specialist can talk you through the options and solutions. You just need to have a general sense of your wishes.

Don't let perfect be the enemy of good. Too many people start working on an estate plan and then get paralyzed by indecision (or spousal disagreement) as they contemplate who would be the best guardian for their children, the best trustee for their kids' assets, and so on and so forth. There is no *best* once you are gone. You're trying to fill a void after the unthinkable has happened. Take your best shot at naming the right folks and move on.

If the attorney who is writing up your estate plan is the same one you hired to do your real estate closing, got you out of a DUI, set up your neighbor's LLC, and is great to call when you have a personal injury claim, find someone else. Estate planning is complicated; you want someone who focuses on it that you can work with over time as your circumstances grow and change. Yes, the basic documents when you are starting out may not be that complicated, but your eventual success will require stronger planning, and you should have that relationship from the get-go. Don't overdo it when choosing a lawyer, though. You don't need to have your plan created by the biggest law firm in town. Yes, it's great to have a specialist with the resources to help you for years and years, but paying skyscraper fees for an estate plan doesn't make sense.

After your plan is created, review it every few years. Send your lawyer an updated net worth statement, have them remind you how the plan works and who you've appointed to positions of responsibility, and make any necessary updates. Beyond this, if you've had a significant change in your life or your net worth, or if the estate tax rules have changed, consider an update meeting.

Also work with someone to assess the life insurance coverage you need. Review the costs and features of different policies, and prioritize term insurance unless there is a strong reason for something else. Pair the life insurance with the right estate planning documents to make sure that your family is well planned for after your death, that your wishes are laid out and followed, that any asset protection or tax-saving techniques are taken advantage of, and that you're not letting your state legislature decide where your assets should go at your death.

Most people do not want to think about dying, which also means that planning for it isn't the hottest topic in the world. Don't be one of those people. The odds are that you will put all of the things discussed in this chapter (and the previous one) into place and live well into old age, but you cannot play the odds with something as important as this.

CHAPTER 12

Protecting Your Portfolio from Yourself

"Don't just do something, stand there!"

—Anonymous investment genius

One of the biggest challenges you'll face as a capital allocator is protecting your capital from yourself. We've already discussed that it's tough to maintain the necessary discipline as a long-term investor to just sit there and do nothing while talking heads blather about the next crisis or the financial news media agitates you with bright yellow and red arrows highlighting market declines. It's hard to stick to your strategy while your nephew is telling you about his Bitcoin profits, your colleague is bragging about his super stock-picking abilities, or your golf buddy regales you with all the right moves his advisor is making. You put a long-term plan in place for a reason. Don't change it out of fear or greed.

We've already reviewed the impact of poor timing decisions on your portfolio in the context of the indexing debate and the client seminars I was involved in. Bad investment-timing decisions can devastate a portfolio, and history shows that investors typically do not perform as well as the strategies in which they are invested.

I'd like to take this topic a bit further, since it should be one of the key takeaways of this book: *How you react to the market could be the most damaging thing you can do to your finances.* The risk you should be worried about isn't market volatility; it's permanently lost capital. It's folly to time your interactions with the market based on forecasts of when it'll be a good or bad time to invest. Let's first look at the risk of market timing to truly hammer this point home. Then we'll wrap up with an analogy that I am hopeful will allow you to put short-term market declines in the proper context.

UNDERSTANDING RISK

Market volatility isn't risk. The word *volatility* carries a negative connotation, but in finance, it's simply a statistical measure of how widely returns are distributed. Upside volatility leads to market gains, which we obviously like. We shouldn't overreact and do dumb things when its evil twin, downside volatility, shows up. Volatility can drive your portfolio higher or lower. Sustained downside volatility can drive it down a lot lower, but the enemy isn't that temporary thrust downward. That happens, and the market and your portfolio can and will recover. The 2007–2009 bear market, which was one of the worst we've ever experienced, bottomed out after approximately eighteen months and recovered fully about three years later.

The real risk to you during this time wasn't the heavy market decline. It was that you made the wrong decision during that decline and turned your short-term loss into a permanent loss of capital by selling out of the market at a low point instead of letting your portfolio recover.

Get out of your own head when you're tempted to either out-think the market or deviate from your plan. You can't time the market. Sorry to spout a cliché, but there's no better way to get this essential point across: Consistent market timing can't be done. You need to understand this when considering how to react to market volatility, because thinking you'll be able to get out and back in at the right time is the most reliable way to turn survivable short-term declines into permanent losses.

A down market sucks. It was absolutely terrifying during the 2007–2009 bear market to see portfolios plummet by more than 50 percent, large institutions collapse, Congress fail to act, a presidential candidate suspend his campaign, hear about a frozen economy with banks that needed to be nationalized, and so on. I get it. I was in living rooms, dining rooms, offices, and conference rooms and on the phone talking to nervous clients. During moments like that, however, or even in less severe declines, deciding that you're going to get out and get back in when things are better is the worst thing you can do.

Unless your situation has changed and you're going to need the money earlier than planned, stick to your portfolio. Any sensible long-term investment strategy was built with the understanding that there would be strong declines multiple times during the portfolio's life. Jumping ship during one doesn't make sense.

The market can't be timed, because we can't accurately forecast when its declines will occur. You may anticipate a decline, bail out, and miss a market gain when that decline never happens or happens when you didn't expect it. You may get out and avoid some of the decline, but there is no way to time the reentry correctly, if you get back in at all. Plenty of investors have been waiting since 2009 for the market to crash again before getting back in.

"We have two classes of forecasters: those who don't know and those who don't know they don't know" is a famous quote by John Kenneth Galbraith, economist and author of *The Great Crash, 1929*.

There's no market guru out there who has consistently been able to tell you when to get out and get back into the market. And I hate to tell you, but you can't do it either. You're either going to believe me on this one, or you're not. To help you decide, let's look at a couple of recent examples.

I started working with a new client in March 2017. At our first meeting, we discussed why he thought it would be a good time to hire an advisor and what his market experience had been. He had tried picking stocks in various ways but ended up losing money on mostly speculation that did not work out. Then he decided to get some help through a brokerage account platform that recommended preferred mutual funds. Invariably, the funds he chose didn't live up to their prior performance, and he got sick of jumping between funds at the wrong time. So he went to Vanguard and plunked his dough into a total stock market index fund.

That was a prudent approach. Forget trying to outsmart the stock market or pick the right funds at the right time; he was just going to take what the market gave him at a very low cost. After all, that's what the financial news media's pseudo intelligentsia has claimed is all anyone needs to do for investing success. It worked quite well. Until it didn't.

A couple of days before election night in November 2016, he became convinced that the market would suffer if Trump won and that, if Clinton prevailed, most of the upside had already been priced in. Politics aside, it was a smart assumption and a somewhat sophisticated analysis. Pollsters had shown that the market had tended to do well over the preceding few months when Clinton's poll numbers were strong and struggled when Trump's numbers rebounded. It became a truism that the market wanted Clinton to win. He sold all of his stocks.

We all know Trump won. We also all know that the market did not tank. It continued its upward climb, and my soon-to-be new client had cost himself an upward move in the market of about 10 percent in only a few months—not to mention having to pay taxes on the capital gains that he generated when he followed his market forecast.

The second example also happened around election time. I was working with a young client who called me up shortly before the election to sell out of the market for the exact same reasons my previous client did. He insisted he wasn't a market timer but that the logic of how the market had moved the last few months made it seem clear that there was little upside and a lot of downside to remaining invested. Once that 10 percent downturn occurred, he would get back in—no harm, no foul.

Let's play this out, I suggested. Let's assume you're right. Trump gets elected and your prediction is correct—the market immediately plummets 10 percent, and there are a ton of news stories explaining why. If I call you up and say it's time to get back in, do you really think you're going to let me reinvest you right there and then? Because I will tell you, you'd be the first client that did.

He agreed. We didn't sell.

STAY THE COURSE

Stick to your plan. Let the portfolio run its course. News events, headlines, economic predictions, and forecasts are a hindrance, not a help to your portfolio.

In a 2016 *MoneyLife* radio interview, Chuck Jaffe talked to Tim Buckley, Vanguard's then chief investment officer and current CEO. Buckley made the claim that "the average investor . . . destroys about 150 [basis points] per year, 1.5 percent a year in return by chasing, by shifting from one type of investment to the next trying to jump around." While Buckley didn't provide the analytics behind this claim, his thought process is similar to what we've been discussing. He counseled investors to change their portfolio "for events in your life, events that are happening with your outlook, not what's going on in China." Your initial portfolio structure was built with the understanding that there would be portfolio volatility. Jumping and running when it materializes doesn't make sense, especially when every portfolio transition results in transaction costs and potential capital gains that will be taxed.

Think of it another way, maybe in a way you've experienced before. Have you ever sold your house? It's usually an emotional process involving many important steps:

- Finding a real estate agent to guide you through a major transaction
- Following their advice on repairs and updates to make the home salable
- Deciding on a listing price after reviewing recent comparable transactions and market availability
- Determining when to list
- Creating the right marketing plan, including a write-up, photos, number of open houses, etc.

Then, the first offer arrives. You had a realistic asking price of $400,000, would have taken a bit less to get a deal done, but your agent breaks the bad news that someone just offered $350,000— 12.5 percent less than what your home is worth.

You're ticked off. You tell your agent that the lowball offer won't work. Not only that, but you won't counter, because the purchaser isn't serious. You're going to be patient and wait for the right offer from a realistic buyer.

I'm not a real estate professional, but I have been involved in enough real estate transactions (and seen clients go through many more) to know that the above scenario happens all the time. Unless they're in a jam, people don't accept lowball offers on their house. They either ignore them or find them offensive and dumb.

So why do people seem to have the exact opposite reaction when the market starts making lowball offers on their portfolio? It's not a perfect analogy, but it's strong enough to illustrate some key similarities.

You meet with a financial advisor and provide summaries of your entire financial life and discuss goals, fears, and plans. You follow their advice and build a financial plan to guide you toward accomplishing important objectives. You set aside enough short-term money in a rainy day fund for emergencies. You decide on an investment mix to grow your portfolio, including what investment philosophy to employ; what mix of stocks, bonds, and other investments to include based on your plan; and which specific investments to use.

You know you won't touch your portfolio for years, perhaps decades, but then the market starts making you crazy, unsolicited offers for it. At least with real estate, your home is for sale when the lowball offer arrives. Your portfolio is not for sale, but the market is quoting you a price on it every second that it's open.

To be fair, the price bounces around a lot, and it's hard to understand why. Reviewing real estate comps and having confidence in what your home is worth are much easier to handle than trying to understand what a portfolio of hundreds if not thousands of underlying investments is worth.

Sometimes you react to the market price offers with amusement, perhaps telling your spouse or best friend how much you're making. Sometimes you react to them with disappointment, hoping the prices will recover but understanding that it's a long-term game.

But when those real lowball offers come in, do you react the same way you would when someone wanted to buy your house for $50,000 less than the asking price? For some reason, we're much more willing to take seriously a market's lowball offer on our portfolio than on our house. We don't get ticked off that the market is trying to scoop up our hard-earned savings cheaply. We don't turn off CNBC because it's not quoting serious prices. We aren't patient; we're stressed. We don't get offended; we get upset. We lose sight of the fact that we have built a thoughtful plan and portfolio strategy and start to give the lowballs much greater power over our financial well-being than they deserve.

Remember that the number of buyers and sellers in the market always matches up (contrary to the silly notion that the market goes down because there are more sellers than buyers). When the market lowballs you, imagine that real estate buyer sliding an offer sheet across your kitchen table trying to buy your brokerage account and 401(k) for less than what they were recently worth—and at a time when they are not for sale! In my imagination, not only do you stick to your plan and say no, but you try and scrape together some cash and see if you can find someone willing to part with their hard-earned investments in this fire sale.

DISCIPLINE

In the long run, markets reward disciplined investors, maybe because that discipline is so hard to maintain in the face of losses and alarming news events. It's difficult to see dollars being lost in your portfolio, but take the long view and understand that, speculation aside, the dollars are only truly lost if you sell and lock in that lower price. In that instance, the market didn't lose that money—your behavior did. The best way to be prepared for a market downturn is to understand that it will happen and that you will ultimately be okay.

Going back to 1980, the stock market has averaged an intrayear decline of 13.9 percent, despite being up twenty-nine out of those thirty-nine years. It's normal for markets to be down 14 percent, because it has happened on average that way for basically the last four decades. When you see a decline of that level, understand that something normal does not have to be reacted to. Volatility is part of the long-term return package of markets.

And yes, we will have much stronger declines, like the 57 percent in the 2007–2009 bear market. But unless you've set yourself up to need that stock money during that decline, you can also successfully ride it out. It'll be harder—infinitely harder, really—than the garden variety 14 percent downturn, but remember that it too will end. By the eighteenth month of the last bear market, the market had started its recovery, and three years after that, you were basically back to even. Stick to your financial plan, because when it comes to market volatility, we haven't seen any other consistent wealth creation approach.

Acknowledgments

This book, and my entire career, would not have been possible without much good luck through the years. I'd like to take this opportunity to thank those that I have had the good fortune of knowing, working with, and learning from during this journey.

I want to thank my beautiful wife, Janine, and my three children, Yasmine, Aden, and Siena, for completing our life. Without Janine, I wouldn't be anywhere close to where I am now. You've made me a better person, and it's been a great ride. To my mom and brother, thanks for always being there for me. Col. Jim Wilson, thank you for planting the seed so many years ago. John Shoro, thank you for being a great mentor in work and life. The team at Heritage Financial, thank you for all that you do for each other and our clients. Chuck Bean and the rest of the Heritage management team, I appreciate your faith in this project and allowing me to pursue it. Jennifer Watson, thanks for your help and flexibility along the way. To the countless clients who have entrusted me with their financial well-being through the years, thank you for your confidence and support.

I'd also like to thank my colleague, Michael Waldron, for his eagle-eyed review of the manuscript, and my good friend, Bill Moore, for helping me conceptualize this idea too many years ago. Finally, thank you to the team at Greenleaf Book Group for their help in making this project a reality. You couldn't have done things any better. In particular, Lindsey, for getting me organized; Nathan and Judy, for improving the message; and Daniel and Jen, for coordinating it all. Others on my Greenleaf team include Danny Sandoval, Olivia McCoy, and Tiffany Barrientos. Thanks so much for your expertise.

About the Author

Sammy Azzouz, JD, CFP®, is president of Heritage Financial Services, based in Westwood, Massachusetts. He is also the author of The Boston Advisor blog (thebostonadvisor.com), which aims to help people who are serious about their finances take their money smarts to the next level.

Sammy has been a wealth manager helping high-net-worth clients achieve their financial and investment goals since 2000. Early in his career, Sammy worked as lead advisor at B&D Advisors, an investment advisory firm run by the estate planning group at the law firm of Bowditch & Dewey, where he drafted estate planning documents, conducted tax research, and worked closely with a robust trust department in addition to his financial planning and investment responsibilities. He then built a national wealth management practice for investment manager Manning & Napier Advisors, where he became one of the youngest and fastest employees to be named a shareholder of that firm. At Manning & Napier, he also served as a portfolio strategist for the firm's dividend-focused investment product.

At Heritage Financial, Sammy works closely with the firm's CEO on all facets of the business. His primary management responsibilities are to help translate Heritage's long-term vision into a strategic direction and to ensure that goals are effectively implemented so the firm can remain at the forefront of delivering high-quality wealth management services to its clients. In addition to his leadership role, he serves as the lead advisor for a select group of high-net-worth clients.

Sammy earned his bachelor of arts from the University of Toronto and his juris doctor from the University of Maryland. After passing the bar in Maryland, he decided to pursue wealth management to help people with all aspects of their finances.

Sammy lives in Millis, Massachusetts, with his wife, Janine, and three children, Yasmine, Aden, and Siena.